LOOSE PARTS

Loose Parts

INSPIRING PLAY IN YOUNG CHILDREN

Lisa Daly and Miriam Beloglovsky ■ Photography by Jenna Daly

Redleaf Press®
www.redleafpress.org
800-423-8309

Published by Redleaf Press
10 Yorkton Court
St. Paul, MN 55117
www.redleafpress.org

First edition 2015
Cover design by Jim Handrigan
Cover and interior photographs by Jenna Daly
Interior design by Erin Kirk New
Typeset in Berkeley Oldstyle and Trade Gothic
Printed in the United States of America
22   21   20   19   18   17   16   15   2   3   4   5   6   7   8   9

Library of Congress Cataloging-in-Publication Data

Daly, Lisa.
  Loose parts : inspiring play in young children / Lisa Daly and Miriam
Beloglovsky ; with photography by Jenna Daly.
     pages cm
  Includes bibliographical references.
  ISBN 978-1-60554-274-4 (pbk. : alk. Paper)
  ISBN 978-1-60554-275-1 (ebook)
1. Play. 2. Early childhood education--Activity programs. 3. Creative
activities and seat work. I. Beloglovsky, Miriam. II. Title.
  LB1139.35.P55D35 2015
  371.21—dc23
                              2014017198

Printed on acid-free paper

To all who value play

To all who tinkered as children

To all who cherish creativity

To all who advocate for preserving childhood

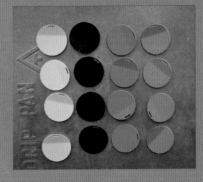

Contents

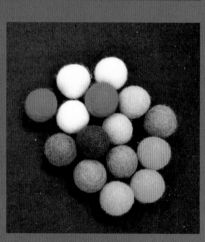

Acknowledgments

We want to extend our deepest appreciation to all of our college students, family members, and friends who share our excitement for loose parts and who continually contribute new ideas and wonderful loose part treasures, many of which are seen in this book. Thank you to Bev Bos and Michael Leeman for their mentoring, friendship, and invaluable inspiration, wisdom, and insight, which sustain our love and passion for providing rich environments for children. This book was enriched by the graphic design expertise of Alexis Baran; the photography, time, and energy of Jenna Daly; the patience, unselfish support, technical skills, and assistance of Dan Daly; and the editing talent of Kyra Ostendorf to make sure the manuscript was just right. And finally, we are grateful to the educators at Folsom Lake College and Solano Community College Children's Program who graciously allowed us to photograph loose parts in their inspirational learning environments.

Part 1
Introduction to Loose Parts

When children interact with loose parts, they enter a world of *"what if"* that promotes the type of thinking that leads to problem solving and theoretical reasoning. Loose parts enhance children's ability to think imaginatively and see solutions, and they bring a sense of adventure and excitement to children's play.

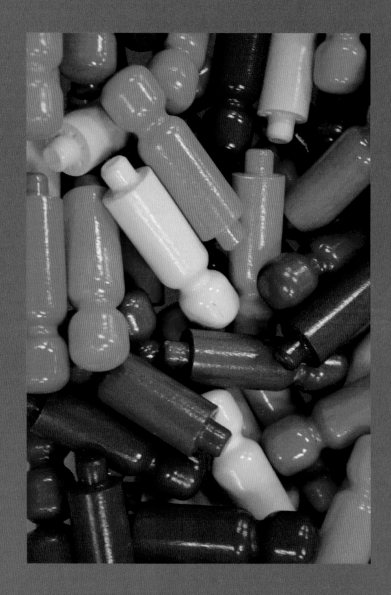

We hope that *Loose Parts* will awaken your creativity and enhance your ability to develop exciting play opportunities for children. Why so many photographs? They're meant to stimulate your imagination and increase your joy in finding loose parts for use in play-based learning.

The before and after photos throughout the book demonstrate loose parts in use throughout early childhood education settings (for example, dramatic play, block/construction, art, language and literacy, math, science, outdoors, sensory, music, and movement). Besides providing challenges, pleasures, and learning opportunities for children, loose parts can also awaken your own creativity. You'll be delighted by finding the perfect loose parts to introduce to children.

As educators, we've certainly taken enormous pleasure in unearthing loose parts for our programs. Over the years, we've stumbled upon an almost limitless variety of treasures. In the aisles of a hardware store, we've found perforated pipes and vinyl gutters perfect for enhancing outdoor play. At a garage sale, we came across a box of old wooden spools that later found a place in our art and block areas. One of our favorite unexpected finds was the set of cow bones we found along a back road. Back at the center, we buried them in the sand of the play yard, where children screamed with excitement while they discovered what they called "dinosaur bones."

What's the source of the joy we experience as we search for these items, think about incorporating our finds into children's play areas, and imagine what the children will do with them? Perhaps we're taken back to our own childhood. We're certain of this: our excitement is contagious, and it's transmitted to the children. Provisioning your setting with loose parts, even though they are humble, can be momentous.

Safety Notes

PVC PIPE
PVC pipe is a useful, inexpensive material to add to your inventory of loose parts. Make sure that the children in your care do not inhale the dust produced by cutting the pipe or lick/mouth the pipe itself.

CHOKING HAZARDS FOR SMALL CHILDREN
Children under the age of three years are likely to explore your collection of loose parts by putting them in their mouths. Please supervise young children closely to prevent choking.

CHAPTER 1
Loose Parts

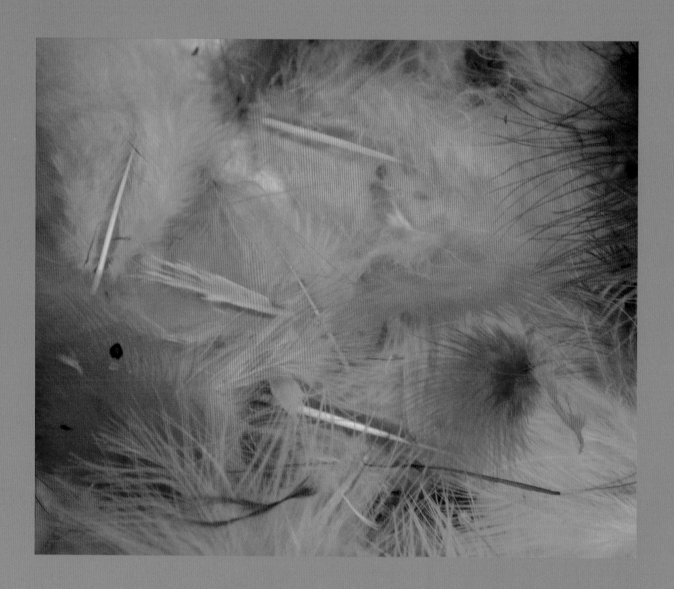

We have often marveled at the long hours children can spend playing with simple materials like boxes, rocks, shells, sand, or water. Our observations have led us to question the conventional wisdom of providing children with sophisticated toys. As you've probably noted yourself, children are often more interested in the packaging than in the toys themselves.

Children usually prefer play that stimulates their curiosity and gives free rein to their imaginations and creativity. We believe that one of the best ways to enhance their natural curiosity is to introduce a wide variety of materials we call "loose parts" into their play settings.

What Are Loose Parts?

In early childhood education (ECE) settings, loose parts mean alluring, beautiful found objects and materials that children can move, manipulate, control, and change while they play (Oxfordshire Play Association, accessed 2014). Children can carry, combine, redesign, line up, take apart, and put loose parts back together in almost endless ways. The materials come with no specific set of directions, and they can be used alone or combined with other materials (Hewes 2006). Children can turn them into whatever they desire: a stone can become a character in a story; an acorn can become an ingredient in an imaginary soup. These objects invite conversations and interactions, and they encourage collaboration and cooperation. Put another way, loose parts promote social competence because they support creativity and innovation. All of these are highly valued skills in adult life today.

Loose Parts Are Captivating

Loose parts are magnets to children, who are naturally curious and gravitate toward novel objects like stones, pinecones, and driftwood. For example, Dylan watched irresistible loose parts spiral from the trees in helicopter fashion. He gathered up the brittle, winged maple seeds and watched them swirl downward when he dropped them from the top of a climbing structure. Later that afternoon, he stuck the seeds straight up like candles in his sand cake. Then he proclaimed them "senshal" (essential) ingredients in dragon brew.

Loose Parts Are Open-Ended

Loose parts possess infinite play possibilities. They offer multiple rather than single outcomes: no specific set of directions accompanies them; no single result is inevitable. Unlike a jigsaw puzzle, whose pieces are meant to be fitted together in a specific way to make a single picture, loose parts can be joined in many

ways. A scarf, for example, can become a blanket to swaddle a baby, a platform for a picnic, a fishing pond, a cover for a fort, or a veil covering the face of a bride.

Loose parts can be taken apart and put back together, combined with other materials, morphed into whatever a child imagines. Blocks can become a tower, then taken apart and made into an enclosure. Stones can be added to the enclosure to serve as food for the farm animals in the block pasture. Next, that block can represent a car or a fish in a pond.

Loose Parts Are Mobile

Loose parts can be easily moved by children while they're playing. For example, Aaron moved driftwood and logs across the play yard to make a fort. Meredith carried acorns from the nature area to the dramatic play area to serve as food for her imaginary puppy.

Origin of Loose Parts

For generations, children have used found materials in their play, from rocks and sticks to tin cans and wire. In his article "How NOT to Cheat Children: The Theory of Loose Parts," the British architect Simon Nicholson coined the term *loose parts* to describe open-ended materials that can be used and manipulated in many ways (1971). Nicholson saw people of every age as potentially creative. Environments, he believed, offer many ways for children to interact with variables such as gravity, sounds, chemical reactions, concepts, words, and people. For Nicholson, the richness of an environment depended on the opportunities it provided for making connections: "In any environment," he wrote, "both the degree of inventiveness and creativity, and the possibility of discovery, are directly proportional to the number and kind of variables in it" (30).

Take, for example, a beach: it is filled with loose parts—rocks, shells, beach glass, plants, feathers. When children play in such a setting, they can move around, making use of any or all of the found objects, devising spaces and structures that can entertain them for hours. This is not only fun but also instrumental in helping them develop higher levels of critical thinking and creativity.

When an environment is rich in loose parts, children are likely to discover multiple ways to manipulate them and new ways of thinking or processing the knowledge learned by playing with the materials. Children can use flat tree cookies to serve as a sturdy base for a tall tower, stepping stones to lead them safely across an imaginary river filled with hungry alligators, a steering wheel for their race car, or a lily pad to shelter frogs. They become more creative and flexible in their thinking while satisfying their ever-growing curiosity and love for learning.

The Value of Loose Parts

Children prefer loose parts. Anyone who has watched children play with toys or playground equipment knows that they quickly tire of things with a sole

purpose. Once they've mastered the key function of an object—pushing the button to make a figure pop up or climbing a ladder, for example—they are ready to move on. The intrigue and the challenge are gone. In other words, children make their play choices based on how much variability those materials offer. A stick is a richer choice than a slide because it can become a fishing pole, a spoon for stirring a concoction, a magic wand, or a balance beam for snails. Loose parts offer almost numberless variables, prompting children to create their own stories.

Loose Parts Promote Active Learning

In their study of loose parts on the playground, Jim Dempsey and Eric Strickland assert that loose parts encourage children to manipulate their environment (1993). According to Dempsey and Strickland, loose parts can be used any way that children choose. Jean Piaget's developmental theory emphasized the need for children to actively manipulate their environments, to experiment, and to interact with materials in order to learn (Piaget 1952). While Piaget did not address loose parts, he believed that children create their own understandings only when they are actively engaged in working with people and objects. Loose parts help children actively construct knowledge from their own experiences. When they can manipulate their own environments and take risks, they are less likely to have accidents and get in trouble. Marc Armitage reported a reduction in minor accidents and a general decline in unwanted behavior with the introduction of loose parts in the play yard (2009). Additionally, children in the study took on more risk and made their own risk assessment, and adult perception of risk changed in a positive way.

Loose Parts Deepen Critical Thinking

Critical thinking investigates, analyzes, questions, and contests beliefs, facts, actions, and information of all kinds. Children learn to use it to challenge assumptions and devise solutions, as Micah, William, and Joe did when they discovered some wooden cove molding, marbles, and Ping-Pong balls that teachers had introduced into the block area as provocations. After figuring out what to do with the materials and trying out their ideas to see what would happen, the boys used the cove molding and some blocks to create inclines and ramps. They experimented with making the marbles roll faster, travel up a ramp, go into containers, and turn corners. The loose parts encouraged the boys to problem solve, make connections, and form relationships.

Loose parts introduce novelty to settings and support cognitively high levels of play (Dodge and Frost 1986). They stimulate children to consider a range of possible uses and meanings for the parts. Once children have exhausted the possibilities in one arrangement, they can rearrange the materials for another game or purpose. By continually rearranging the loose parts, they create settings that match their own skills. When they have plenty of loose parts to manipulate, children seldom become bored. Their problem-solving skills and imaginations are increased by multipurpose loose parts. They build knowledge through exploring the objects in the world around them (Kamii and DeVries 1993).

Loose Parts Promote Divergent and Creative Thinking

In a keynote speech on September 20, 2012, Paul Collard observed that young children today will work in careers that haven't been invented yet. Similarly, Karl Fisch in a "Did You Know?" presentation stated, "We are currently preparing students for jobs that don't yet exist, using technologies that haven't been invented, in order to solve problems we don't even know are problems yet" (Fisch and

McLeod 2012). This may be difficult for any of us to grasp, but think of the current technologies that didn't exist fifteen years ago: iPods, smartphones, tablet computers, MP3s, nanotechnology. To meet the challenges and opportunities of the future, today's children must become critical and creative thinkers, intelligent problem solvers, and good communicators. These skills develop when they tinker with loose parts. Consider children's play as they engage with commercially made materials found in a child development center such as a vehicle in a block area or plastic food in a dramatic play area. An ambulance or plastic peas remain the same items as intended by the toy manufacturer; no imagination is required. If, however, a child is given driftwood, he can transform the wood into any vehicle or food he desires: a race car or an airplane, a fire or garbage truck, sushi or spaghetti. In fact, he can use his imagination and critical thinking to have the wood represent anything he wishes.

Children's creativity and problem solving lead to the deeper critical thinking skills they'll need to succeed as adults (Asbury and Rich 2008). "The divergent thinking of creative children is fluent, flexible, original, and elaborate" (Fox and Schirrmacher 2012, 23). Loose parts encourage diverse thinking, thanks to their open-endedness. (For a wonderful example of childlike creativity, read Antoinette Portis's *Not a Box*, whose rabbit hero discovers that a cardboard box can become a rocket ship, a race car, a boat, a robot, and a hot air balloon, among other things.)

Loose Parts Support Developmental Domains

Developmental literature on the role of play is explicit: play stimulates physical, social-emotional, and cognitive development in children's early years (Brown 2009; Johnson, Christie, and Wardle 2005; Shonkoff and Phillips 2000; Sluss 2005). Developmental theory emphasizes the need for children to manipulate their environments in order to learn (Piaget 1952; Vygotsky 1967; Dewey 1990). Children build on their existing knowledge, and to do so, they must interact with their environments. Loose parts provide them with many opportunities to handle, build, rebuild, and re-create their ideas and experiences and to grow across all of the developmental domains.

PHYSICAL DEVELOPMENT

Between three and six years, children rapidly acquire new gross- and fine-motor skills. Activities using loose parts help them develop confidence in their ability to use their bodies for their own purposes. For example, children gain self-assurance as they climb, step, jump, and balance from tree stump to tree stump. During this phase, children become aware of their bodies' positions in space, including how to move cautiously when constructing a fort or climbing on large wooden spools to attach ropes to a tree branch. Small loose parts like shells, stones, corks, and craft sticks help them develop their small muscles and hand-eye coordination. Children need ample opportunities to manipulate a range of materials to develop their fine-motor skills (Copple and Bredekamp 2009).

SOCIAL-EMOTIONAL DEVELOPMENT

Loose parts also support children's sense of belonging, their inclusiveness, their willingness to take risks, and their passion—all critical elements in social-emotional development. While these characteristics may be evident as a result of children's engagement in different school experiences, activities and materials that are diverse, open-ended, and unstructured best nurture children's social-emotional growth. Marc Armitage assessed the effectiveness of a pilot study in the United Kingdom involving the introduction of loose parts into primary

school play yards during lunchtime. The study revealed that providing loose parts significantly enhanced inclusion for all children and helped improve children's relationships and self-confidence. Additionally, play with loose parts increased children's collaboration, negotiation skills, risk taking, conflict resolution, communication, and problem solving. Adults reported that children engaged with loose parts were more occupied, had fewer disputes, and had less bad behavior than with the school's traditional play yard equipment. Interestingly, the study also found that the adults had a better experience with their school day (Armitage 2009).

Our experience observing different types of early learning environments also illustrates the influence and impact of loose parts on children's social competency. One center type consists of typical play equipment: climbing structure, play house, tricycles, balls, and lots of room to run; all appropriate equipment for a center. These environments, however, are mainly dominated by children's loud arguments, physical aggression, and inappropriate language. The teachers constantly assist with behavior challenges. Many children just run around and do not get involved in any activity, but if they do, they stay for only a brief time. Another center type has outdoor play areas filled with natural loose parts. The children's quality of play is strikingly different. Children collaborate on using palm fronds for building forts, logs and eucalyptus bark to make enclosures, and tree cookies and rocks in dramatic play. The environment is filled with children's laughter, invitations to join, shared purpose, and investigation. Teachers spend time in meaningful conversations with children and supporting children's play. Our conclusion is that loose parts enhance social-emotional growth through deeper play while close-ended materials designed to be used in uniform or pre-scribed ways limit play potential.

Learning to take risks is crucial to young children's social-emotional development. Julia took a risk when she dragged a wooden plank over to the sandbox and angled it from the sandbox's edge to the grass. Then she grasped the plank's edges and pulled herself cautiously up her ramp in a bear walk. She shouted to Stephen, "Hey, don't come over here, or you'll be in lava!"

Children benefit from taking risks in play; being overprotected can inhibit their development (Gleave 2008). When working with open-ended materials like loose parts, children take risks in moving their bodies and learning to challenge their own strength and ability.

Passion, another element in social-emotional development, fuels children's intense liking for or interest in activities, objects, or concepts. Lizzy and Tanner

were passionate about potions. Each day, they darted out to the play yard, following the crushed granite path to the back corner. There, their mixing began. They filled empty kitchen pots and pans with overflowing scoops of dirt and gravel, dumped water in the dirt, turned it to mud, and then sprinkled handfuls of dried grass on top. Their play continued for several weeks while they experimented with different ingredients and made endless mud pies. Lizzy and Tanner were doing what interested, engaged, and motivated them. Open-ended materials sparked their passion. Loose parts fed their fervor for reencountering and transforming familiar materials. Zeal like theirs leads to commitment and can be shared with others. Everyone learns better when driven by passion.

Nothing gives children a greater sense of power than being in control of the materials they're using. Because loose parts are open-ended, children can make choices and decisions about how to use them—and learning to choose well is part of social-emotional development. On a chilly November morning, we

watched a group of children gather around a heaped pile of dirt in the play yard left behind by contractors building a new patio. Our first inclination was to remove the dirt, but as we watched the children, we realized the play potential of that mound. The dirt hill was a loose part. The children added their own materials of sticks to dig, acorns to bury, and cardboard for sliding. It still beckons children today to play King of the Hill, unearth their own buried treasures, dig to China, and slide down the hill on their bottoms and cardboard—all play activities that bestow power.

Children feel productive when they accomplish something, when their work is valued, and when they do not feel a sense of failure. When they're engaged in a project, time doesn't matter. Working with loose parts teaches them that their work has merit. Jasmine and Gracie stumbled across fairy dust outside the art room door one day, and that's when their quest to build a fairy house began. Convinced that the glitter in the sand had been left by frolicking fairies, the girls decided to create a magical dwelling for them. They spent days enthusiastically discussing what fairies needed in a home. They drew up plans, collected materials, sawed wood, and constructed the house. They painted wallpaper with a light, lacy design, added walnut shell beds, and left ribbons so the fairies could dance. And each evening, the fairies sprinkled the house with fairy dust as proof of their pleasure in their new home. The teachers supported Jasmine and Gracie's work by giving the girls space, time, and materials to pursue their endeavor. The teachers' actions showed that they valued the girls' work.

COGNITIVE DEVELOPMENT

This concerns *how* children learn rather than *what* they learn. It includes critical thinking, language, concept of number, classification, spatial relationships, representations of experiences and ideas, and solving problems. According to Jean Piaget, children construct their own knowledge out of their direct experiences (Piaget 1973).

Children use loose parts to acquire, organize, and apply learning. By physically manipulating loose parts, they learn about the objects and the relationships between them while developing problem-solving skills. Beginning levels of critical thinking, like remembering and understanding, are enhanced when children recall when and where they have seen sand, discover what can be done with it, and understand that dry and wet sand have different properties. When children add to their knowledge of sand by pouring water on it to make it more moldable, they advance to a higher level of critical thinking involving abstraction. As they describe sand and their experiences with it, their language skills develop. When they can understand *more* and *less sand* and can count shells in the sand, the concept of number becomes real to them. Classification starts to become meaningful when children organize shells into like groups. Spatial relationships are supported when children sit or stand while digging in and moving around mounds of sand. Representations of ideas become embodied when they make a sand castle and surround it with a moat. Problem-solving skills come into play whenever children experiment with loose parts.

Sunana, Patrick, and Maddie picked up a six-foot-long wooden plank. Sunana and Patrick lifted from one side and Maddie from the other. They shuffled along a concrete path bordered by a foot-high retaining wall until they came to a halt where the path bent to the left; they were unable to maneuver the turn with their long plank. They reversed their steps and tried again and again. Sunana suggested that they grasp the board from below and hold it up high. This strategy wasn't successful. At last, Maddie moved to the same side of the board as the other two children. Whether her move was intended to solve the problem or not, it worked. The children could now navigate the turn. A loose part had led them to solve a complex spatial problem.

Loose Parts Are Developmentally Inclusive

Children of all ages, abilities, skill levels, and genders can use loose parts successfully. Because there's no right or wrong way to work with them, all children can achieve competence, build on existing strengths, and feel successful and independent.

Because loose parts are so open-ended, they can support play for children of every cultural background, class, ability, and gender—but only if you choose them wisely. As a teacher, you're responsible for selecting materials that do not promote stereotypes. Here's an example: when we were writing this book, we carefully considered every loose part we hoped to include in it. We did not

include boxes with commercial advertising on them because introducing a Cheerios box to the dramatic play area might be hard on a child whose family could not afford to buy brand-name cereal. We also wanted to be thoughtful about not using items in possibly disrespectful ways with symbolic meaning in specific cultures. For example, we discussed using chopsticks as building materials but decided not to because we wanted to respect chopsticks' role as valued eating tools in some Asian cultures. As an ECE teacher, you want to celebrate diversity and promote equality in your classroom. One way to do that is to choose loose parts that reflect and honor diversity and that don't stereotype.

Loose Parts Promote a Wide Range of Play

Early childhood education teachers know that children learn through self-directed play. This kind of play is complex, pleasurable, self-motivated, imaginative, spontaneous, creative, and happily free of adult-imposed goals and outcomes. Children determine and control the content of this play, following their own instincts, ideas, and interests (Playwork Principles Scrutiny Group 2005). Loose parts engage children in play involving their entire selves. Sara Smilansky proposed that functional, constructive, and dramatic play categories represent a continuum of children's increasing cognitive abilities; how children use play materials can be used to assess their development (1968).

FUNCTIONAL PLAY

Functional play explores what objects are like and what can be done with them.
For example, Javon spent an entire week exploring colored glass stones. He ran

his fingers through them, poured them from container to container,
and lined them up in straight rows. He eventually sorted and classified
them, first by color and then by mixing similar colors. He created patterns: green, blue, green, blue. His combinations could be repetitive
or random, and he commented on what colors looked best together.
One Monday when he arrived at school, he went directly to the library.
He selected a book with the work of the painter Piet Mondrian. Using
sticks and his colored glass stones, Javon re-created Mondrian's color
blocks inside a picture frame. His activity now had a new purpose. His creations
were constructive play. The combinations he selected were intentional; we could
tell that he had been practicing with a specific plan in mind.

CONSTRUCTIVE PLAY

Children engage in constructive play when they create something new using
existing play objects. Diego, who was skilled at building complex structures
with blocks and Legos, encountered a new set of loose plastic connectors. He
started arranging them by shape and testing the many possibilities they offered.
He constructed what appeared to be a large, towerlike structure. As it grew taller,
he added other parts that he identified as the arms and legs of his robot. Eventually, he figured out a way to make the arms move. He played with this robot for
a long time, along with other children. Building robots went on for weeks, and
more loose parts became used in different parts of the setting.

DRAMATIC AND SYMBOLIC PLAY

Dramatic play is particularly important for social-emotional and cognitive development (Vygotsky 1967; Pepler and Rubin 1982; Rubin 1982). Donna M. Bagley
and Patricia H. Klass also support the importance of symbolic play and suggest
that the quality of play objects can affect dramatic and symbolic play. In many
cases, the more open-ended and ambiguous those objects are, the better they
function (1997). For example, Alejandro had recently been hospitalized with
asthma. When he returned to school, he spent a lot of time re-creating his hospital experience through symbolic play. He built his hospital with blocks and tree
cookies, making it bigger and bigger. Charlotte and David joined him in

building it and took on the roles of doctor and nurse. They playacted the experiences Alejandro had endured in the hospital. Rocks became pretend medication, plastic tubing attached to a shoe box became a breathing machine, and a plastic connector became Alejandro's inhaler. This play went on for weeks. Eventually the children gravitated to other areas of play after Alejandro had relived his traumatic experience in a gentle way.

Loose Parts Are Sustainable and Economically Feasible

With so many materials available for ECE classrooms, you need to make choices that maximize children's development and make sense financially. Today teachers are often expected to provide classroom materials out of their own pockets. Happily, loose parts can often be had for free, and they offer a bonus: they encourage you, and the children's parents, to reuse, renew, and recycle. Write a note to the children's families asking them to collect potentially rich materials around their homes to add to the classroom. Provide a list of suggested items (small boxes, jar lids, buttons, fabric). Also, post it in the classroom or distribute it at school events.

Loose Parts Support the Curriculum

Loose parts offer many possibilities for open-ended learning. Especially in ECE programs where standards and ditto sheets are threatening to take over, advocate for loose parts as supports for the acquisition of skills that children are required to demonstrate when they enter kindergarten.

MATH

Children acquire their first math skills and understanding of numerical concepts when they manipulate small loose parts, like blocks and bottle caps, by sorting

and classifying and combining and separating them. They learn one-to-one correspondence when they make connections among loose parts. Once they begin integrating loose parts into their games, you commonly hear them start to count and see them arranging the parts in specific sequences, patterns, and categories by color, type, number, and class. Loose parts lend themselves to classification. The concept of measurement becomes clear when children play with tools like cups, sticks, funnels, and sifters. Measurement, equivalency, balance, spatial awareness, conservation, and logical classification are precursors to higher mathematical skills that loose parts readily support.

PHYSICAL SCIENCE

Loose parts help children investigate and actively construct ideas and explanations about physical properties of the nonliving world. Children gain deeper knowledge of how things work when they can experiment with stacking boxes, tubes, and bottles. They can also test multiple hypotheses involving gravity, force, weight, distance, and height with these materials. Children learn that things move in many various ways (motion) through playing with loose parts that can be pulled and pushed to start, stop, or change their movement. Wooden boards, gutters, and balls help them investigate inclines and gravity. Prisms and open-ended materials that are transparent, translucent, or opaque on a light table or overhead projector help children experiment with color, shadows, and reflected or refracted light. Magnetic and nonmagnetic loose parts made of wood, metal, paper, or plastic help children learn that magnets attract some objects but repel others. Sound (pitch and volume) is explored as items of various shapes, sizes, and materials are played with in water, air, and sand. Metal cans, coconut shells, bamboo sticks, cardboard tubes, and stones are good examples. Using loose parts to explore bubbles assists children in learning about air. A variety of objects such as strawberry baskets, sifters, Mason jar lid rings, and funnels make interesting bubbles.

DRAMATIC AND SYMBOLIC PLAY

Loose parts encourage dramatic and symbolic play, indoors and out. These materials offer children the chance to embody the worlds of their imaginations and to create complex stories and scripts assisted by props. Stones become roads and homes for pets and pretend families. Tree branches serve as supports for imaginary campfires and roasting marshmallows. Loose parts offer children opportunities to understand their past experiences and to engage in realistic, complex representations of their daily lives. Such objects keep them in the present, test multiple ideas and possibilities for future use, and stimulate children to plan and communicate their plans to other children and adults (Bretherton 1998; Singer, Golinkoff, and Hirsh-Pasek 2006).

LANGUAGE AND LITERACY

Stan Kuczaj's research stresses the relationship between spontaneous play and language and literacy development, arguing that all four aspects of human language systems (phonological, syntactic, semantic, and pragmatic) become incorporated into young children's play (Kuczaj 1985). Loose parts promote language development when children use them as props to engage in rich conversations and storytelling with peers and adults. Describing the items they manipulate, children can test new, complex words and engage in productive arguments that increase their critical-thinking skills. They make connections between loose parts, the books they have read, and the stories they have heard. They use loose parts to plan and draw their ideas and interactions (Bohling, Saarela, and Miller 2010). Ample, continuous use of loose parts helps children improve their memories, vocabularies, and literacy.

ART

Children often express their ideas and feelings through art. An open art studio offers them tools and materials for telling their stories. Adding loose parts to the art area can enhance their creativity and help them extend their ideas and questions. Friedrich Froebel, the father of the kindergarten movement, argued that young children benefit from making their own art and enjoying the art of others. He considered art activities important parts of supporting the "full and all-sided development of children" (Froebel 2005). When loose parts are added to your art center, they offer children invitations to draw, sculpt, collage, explore, and extend their ideas. Such opportunities shouldn't be confined to the art area, though. Fill your indoor and outdoor settings with open-ended resources to encourage creative expression everywhere. Children's sense of beauty can be as easily seen in their arrangements of sticks lined up side by side, wooden planks propped symmetrically against a lodge, rock mosaics laid in sand, and pinecones arranged in spirals.

SENSORY EXPLORATION

Young children learn through their senses. Sight, sound, touch, smell, and taste are how they initially make sense of the world around them. Loose parts nurture their sensory play—think about the stunning colors of natural materials like moss, tree bark, and seashells. Stones click together and blocks crash down. When children play with water and open-ended materials, they learn about the sound and weight of poured water, about filling up a bottle, and about making bubbles. Children's capacity for touch is deepened when they experience the tactile qualities of objects that are rough, smooth, prickly, spongy, wet, furry, fuzzy, bumpy, slick, abrasive, hard, and soft. Their sense of smell develops when they are exposed to fragrant loose parts like herbs, cocoa mulch, spices, pinecones, dry leaves, and flowers. Because hands-on experiences with materials are critical to early learning, it's important to include sensorily challenging and pleasing loose parts in your ECE setting.

MOVEMENT AND MUSIC

Music and movement capture children's attention and hearts. Much movement for children takes place through self-directed, self-initiated play as they freely move their bodies (Edwards, Bayless, and Ramsey 2009). Movement possibili-

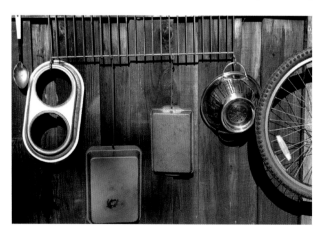

ties with loose parts such as scarves, hoops, and ribbons are endless and provide opportunity for children to improvise. Musical play often means hitting items as hard as possible to see how they sound, and loose parts offer almost limitless opportunities to explore sounds that can be exuberant, random, noisy, and chaotic or quiet, gentle, and focused. Almost all children will naturally have the ability to interact with music (Miché 2002). The teacher's role is to provide a music environment to support the development of a child's musical ability. Musical concepts in early childhood are not initially taught in a highly structured manner but are learned gradually over a period of time (Edwards, Bayless, and Ramsey 2009). Children develop a sense of rhythm as they beat a variety of different loose parts such as rhythm sticks made of bamboo, wood, plastic, or metal. They may bang on various drum surfaces from metal cans to five-gallon buckets and tree stumps. Many people have memories of using loose parts for banging (metal pots and pans with wooden spoons) in the kitchen as children. Loose parts support movement and music making across all of the developmental domains: physical, social-emotional, and cognitive.

Loose Parts in Outdoor Settings

When children play outdoors, their opportunities with loose parts increase dramatically. They find wonder in leaves, sticks, rocks, and other natural objects. Stones on the road or in the garden mesmerize them. These stones may become a campfire, watering hole for animals, or dragon eggs when children reenact a story they've heard.

Current research demonstrates that children engage in more creative forms of play in green areas than in manufactured play areas (Louv 2008). Loose parts including branches, rocks, wood, dirt, water, sand, and bark support play and provide unending creative exploration in an outdoor environment. The high levels of complexity and variety that nature offers invite longer and more complex play (White and Stoecklin 2014). Richard Louv states, "Nature, which excites all the senses, remains the richest source of loose parts" (2008, 87).

· ·

We hope that you are inspired by this book to add more loose parts to children's play. When you provide loose parts and have an open mind about how they may be used, the children will surprise and delight you with what they create and learn.

Part 2
Senses

I hear and I forget.

I see and I remember.

I do and I understand.

CONFUCIUS

Color

Texture

Sound

Our senses allow us to learn, to grow, to feel, to protect ourselves, and to enjoy our world.

Children have an amazing sense of wonder and curiosity. They are in a constant journey of discovery and exploration to understand how things work and function. From birth, children are experts at using their senses to learn about the world. Heightening each one of their senses strengthens the neuronal pathways and opens a window to make connections to previous knowledge and learning. Thoughtfully planned sensory play experiences support children's innate curiosity, while allowing them to fully use their senses: hearing, seeing, tasting, smelling, and touching.

Loose parts provide multiple opportunities to engage the senses by encouraging children's curiosity and respecting their ways of learning about the world. Incorporating natural materials such as pinecones, acorns, sycamore pods, rocks, and stones into sand, Jurassic sand, or mud add texture to heighten the sense of touch. A sound garden with multiple cans, bells, and pots and pans to bang and create sound raises the sense of hearing. Colorful scarves, leaves, and balls of various colors enhance children's sense of sight. There is nothing like playing with meaningful materials and experiences to stimulate the senses.

CHAPTER 2

Color

Color is the way that children make distinctions about things they see in their environment. They show delight in naming colors as they use bottle caps for making designs or when they watch colorful bottles floating in the water. Loose parts found in nature offer a palette that is always changing, from the beauty of fall colored leaves to the winter blues of sea glass and to spring and summer flowers. Children enjoy mixing colors with translucent loose parts on a light table. They comment about the many color combinations when they design with tiles, marbles, and beads. When children explore paint swatches, they can match similar colors and create a sequence or "color train" of hues from light to dark.

Children use color as a means for defining and organizing their world. Color represents feelings and emotions. Yellow ribbons are warm and happy. Blue beads are peaceful and deep. Green leaves represent nature and stillness. Red marbles are glowing and confident. Orange jewels are radiant and healthy. Designing and creating art with colorful loose parts help children express their feelings. Loose parts offer multiple possibilities to explore color.

The Many Colors of Light

While playing outdoors, the children notice a series of bright spots bouncing on the wall. They immediately begin to speculate about what is causing them. Genevive says, "I think the sun is changing colors." Tomas answers, "The sun is not many colors; it is only yellow. Don't you see the painting?" (referring to a series of artwork portraying the sun in bright yellows). The teachers want to encourage children to find the source of the light spots, so they invite the children to walk around to see if they can find shiny objects that make light. The teachers move the colorful mirror tiles placed on one of the tables. Sandra looks at the mirrors and says, "Look, it's coming from here," as she moves the mirror. All the children get a mirror and begin to move it around, making the light spots bounce. This simple discovery triggers a series of hypotheses that leads to a complex investigation of light, reflection, and color brightness. Prisms are added to the environment. The children play and explore them for days. To add to the investigation, the teachers turn the light table on and set up a series of colorful provocations, including translucent and opaque beads, cups, and acrylic cylinders. The teachers also incorporate natural loose parts, such as leaves, for children to explore and notice the variety of shades the leaves have to offer. This purposeful and intense work continues for days, and the children's questions guide them into new discoveries about color.

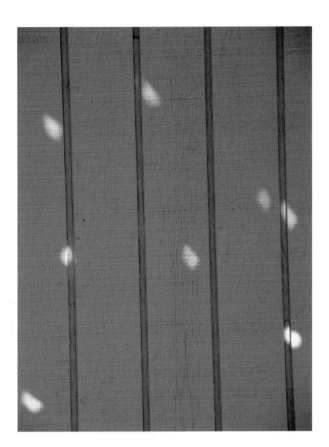

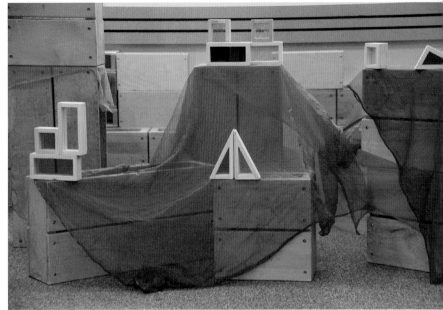

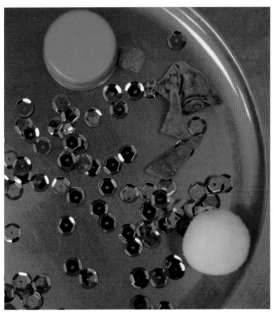

Primary colors are the three main colors—red, blue, and yellow—that can be mixed together to create other colors. Sam looks over the intriguing collection of colorful collage materials. He runs his hands over the light, medium, and dark shades of green, blue, and purple items. He picks up dark cobalt-blue sea glass and a green bottle cap and randomly places the items on a bright red tray. He grasps a fistful of green sequins. He opens his fingers, and the sequins randomly fall on his design. "Look, it's raining green sparkles!" Next he takes two small yellow pom-pom balls, stretches his right hand up high, and drops the balls one at a time onto his design. "Watch out below! Here come the yellow ones."

A shade of color can be created by adding black paint or a tint of color created by adding white paint to the original color. Children learn about the various shades of one color by sorting and classifying fall leaves. Jenny discovers that there are many shades of orange (her favorite color) as she arranges the fall leaves in a design.

Analogous colors are groups of colors that are adjacent to each other on the color wheel. Shelton describes his elaborate tile design by saying, "This is green and goes next to the blue, because they look good together." He has learned that analogous colors enhance his designs.

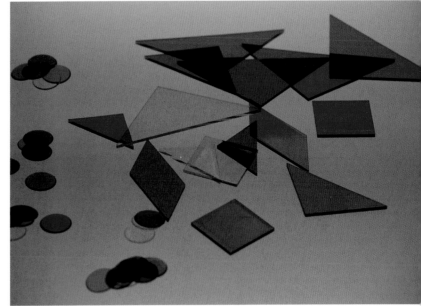

Bright colors are defined by the amount of light that is reflected in large amounts. Children can explore bright colors by playing with prisms and flashlights reflected in both opaque and translucent loose parts. As Tomas bounces the light off a blue gemstone, he exclaims, "Look, it is brighter." He then removes the light and comments on how the color changes and becomes dull or soft.

Secondary colors are the colors obtained when two primary colors are mixed together. Children can explore mixing primary colors to create other colors. Tammy uses an eyedropper to squeeze a few drops of red watercolor into the yellow watercolor. "I see that red and yellow make orange." She continues to combine watercolors to make new colors.

CHAPTER 3

Texture

Texture is the tactile quality of the surface of an object or a work of art. It is the way an object feels when it is touched. Texture is a source of interest and information. It also denotes space and changes in areas of an object or environment. Loose parts offer children multiple possibilities to use their sense of touch and engage in spontaneous exploration. Texture can be added to the environment in the form of sand, pebbles, leaves, grass, fabric, ribbon, papers, and stones, just to name a few. Each of these materials offers children a unique texture: prickly, knobby, soft, silky, and rough, among others.

Children are known for touching everything. They explore objects using their sense of touch and learn much about the world through their hands. When observing children, we can see them reaching for natural items such as pinecones and acorns. They enjoy caressing smooth objects such as blankets or satin fabrics. They love to get their hands wet and touch rocks and marbles. They play with grass, flowers, and pine needles. Children enjoy going on nature walks, which offer them opportunities to encounter a range of textures in natural found objects. Often that first touch leads to further explorations.

A Squishy City

On a hot summer day, the sprinklers are turned on to encourage children to engage in water play and stay cool. Russel, Shawn, and Delicia are excited to discover that the sprinkler created something new—mud. They cannot resist touching and jumping in the mud. Their conversation describes the various textures they encounter. Shawn says, "See, it's smooth and slimy." Delicia responds, "It's cold too." Their play continues and they start to incorporate different rocks and pebbles. Russel shouts, "I can build something with the mud." The children agree and they start looking for twigs and branches. The children continue to build and to add more loose parts until the mud puddle turns into what they call "a squishy city."

Tactile is what we perceive by touching an object. Natural objects have different textures. They are silky like the petals of a flower or a smooth leaf. They can be prickly like a sycamore pod or bumpy like the top of an acorn. Jenna pokes varying sizes of acorns and acorn caps into a large ball of moist clay. On the top of the clay ball, she inserts stiff seed pods and rough pieces of bark that radiate straight up from the clay ball toward the ceiling. She carefully picks up a prickly sycamore ball with her index finger and thumb and presses it into the soft clay. She continues to work silently as she pushes more items into the clay.

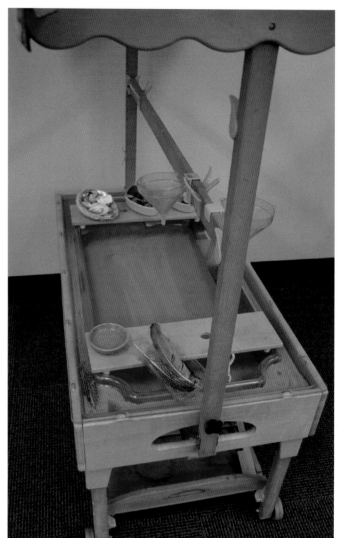

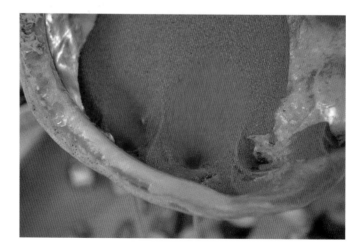

Natural textures are from anything found in nature, such as flower petals, twigs, leaves, acorns, pinecones, and buckeyes. Natural items offer an incredible opportunity to experience texture. Combined with Jurassic sand, moon sand, cocoa mulch, mud, and beach sand they become stimulating sensory experiences for children to explore. Teddy uses an abalone shell as a tool to scoop up the Jurassic sand. His eyes fixate on the rusty sand disappearing through the shell's holes and spilling onto the sand and tree cookies in the sensory table.

Artificial textures are from anything created by a human being, such as plastic, paper, and metal. Bottle caps can be sorted and classified by both texture and color. Cardboard, card stock, and handmade paper can be used to create art with implied texture. Ellen uses her hands to smooth out fabric samples on the block area platform. She begins in a corner and meticulously continues until the entire platform is covered with fabric in a geometric pattern.

CHAPTER 4

Sound

Young children are often quick to pick up on new sounds in their environment, and they typically enjoy and are intentional in making music. They differentiate between musical sounds and adapt them to create a specific rhythm or pitch. They move their bodies as they explore sound, thus realizing that touch and movement change the sound they produce. Children are fascinated by all types of sounds, from water flowing in a water wall to the sound they make when banging a pot or pan. Sound gives children the opportunity to develop listening skills, understand scientific concepts, and explore their own sound and music-making abilities. Sound offers children a vehicle for self-expression.

Loose parts provide children with multiple opportunities to create sound and music. They support the whole child and children's desire to use language and body movement to express their ideas. Creating a sound garden invites exploration. Banging on a variety of pots, pans, bells, and metal trays allows children to release their emotions. Children differentiate between different tones as they bang on wood boxes or metal cans.

Adding cardboard egg cartons along with wooden spoons helps children explore flat sounds. Aluminum pie plates are fun to bang together. Aluminum foil creates various sounds. It can be laid on the floor for children to walk on or they can tap their fingers on it to create a rainstorm. Children can work together to shake it and make little and big sounds. Walnut or coconut shells can be banged together to make the sound of horses walking. Children run rhythm sticks and kitchen utensils back and forth on corrugated cardboard or pipe. Coffee cans are an easy way to introduce children to bass sounds. Loose parts provide endless possibilities to create sound and music.

Noah Explores Sound

Today Noah sits in the same place for a long time, experimenting with the sounds that the pots, pans, and kitchen utensils make. He carefully revisits each loose part and makes various sounds by banging the objects together. He laughs at the loud bang a metal spoon

makes when he hits a metal lid. Noah spends time exploring a wooden spoon; he moves it around and hits it on the ridges of a corrugated coffee can. He uses his hand to bang down on a metal bowl and makes consistent rhythms as if he were banging on a drum. He uses a metal container and a small wooden container, banging the spoon inside both containers, and carefully listens to the various sounds he is making.

Later in the day, Noah spends time exploring the variety of sounds he can make in the sound garden. He goes from the cans to the bells and bangs them with gusto. He dances when other children drum on a trash can lid.

Pitch is the sensation made by various musical instruments, in which musical tones are assigned to relative positions on a musical scale. For instance, banging on metal buckets can produce a high pitch, while banging on plastic buckets can produce a lower pitch. Jonathon uses rhythm sticks to drum on the ten-gallon bucket while Sukie uses fleece-covered mallets to pound on the galvanized tub.

Timbre is the character or quality of a musical sound or voice. Stretched strings on a frame allow children to create sounds and differentiate between various timbres. Cans suspended from string have a different timbre than cans placed on a flat surface. Bells of various sizes create a wide variety of timbres that children can explore. Sarah strikes the tin cans with a large metal serving spoon and then hits the metal pipes to compare sounds.

Rhythm is a regular repeated pattern of sounds. Aaliyah brings a thick dowel to the sand area and buries one half into the sand. She puts a big pot on top of the dowel, grabs a couple of spoons, and starts banging on the pot. Other children join and bang on pans, large buckets, and small cans. They try different rhythms and they follow each other's lead. Aaliyah says, "We are a band and we create music."

Intensity is defined as sound power; it can be high or low, loud or soft. To help children compare sound, Lisa sets up bowls of pebbles, acorns, and sycamore balls for the children to make their own sound shakers. Children fill clear plastic boxes with the natural materials and compare the intensity of the sound produced. As they shake each box, the natural materials make their own unique sound.

Part 3
Creativity

Creativity is inventing, experimenting, growing, taking risks, breaking rules, making mistakes, and having fun.

MARY LOU COOK

Art

Design

Symbolic Play

Creativity is the ability to see things differently, think divergently, create something unique, and solve problems. It involves the skill of creating something new or combining things in new but meaningful ways.

Children's creative expression is seen through art, music, imaginative play, and dance as they paint, sculpt, drum, role-play, and move. It is also visible in construction, science, mathematics, writing, and cooking as children build with blocks, dictate a story, or make a concoction. Creativity or originality is revealed as children experiment and combine materials in unique, unexpected, and interesting ways. According to J. P. Guilford, traits of a creative child include curiosity, flexibility, sensitivity, persistence, divergent thinking, and risk taking (1967). Every child possesses a creative spirit that will either blossom when nurtured or wither if stifled. The key to developing creativity in children is to heighten awareness and provide inspiration.

Loose parts promote creativity and divergent thinking. Creating art and designing with a variety of loose parts stimulates children's curiosity and inventiveness. It allows them to think outside the box and gives free rein to their imagination and creativity. A box becomes a canvas to paint or a sculpture to build. Pebbles turn into treasure. Colorful tiles can be arranged to create intricate designs. The open-ended quality of loose parts supports children to make choices, take risks, and become fluid thinkers. These are all important qualities of a creative person. With loose parts, children can create, design, and enter the world of symbolic play without the constraints of having to create a final product and without judgment. In symbolic play, children creatively use loose parts to make soup and build forts, homes, and quiet spaces. They use scarves to become "superheroes" or put together a full orchestra by inventing their own instruments. In other words, creativity enhances all aspects of children's experience.

CHAPTER 5

Art

Art inspires children to create and use their imagination. True art for young children involves an open-ended, unstructured, and creative process. It is process-oriented rather than product-oriented, which means that children can explore and experiment with art materials as they desire rather than duplicate a given pattern. Art is child-centered rather than teacher-directed so that children have opportunities to use art materials freely in their own creative, original, and unique ways. The concept of art is broader than art tools and supplies and includes loose parts. Loose parts such as glass stones and tiles, seashells and glass, and pebbles, twigs, and leaves enhance creative art development when children can manipulate materials and tinker with them. Children's creativity increases when they have large blocks of uninterrupted time to express their artistic ideas with loose parts.

Children are often seen moving objects and arranging them in complex patterns. Loose parts are a perfect medium to encourage children to engage in art. They can be moved and organized to create multiple expressions of children's thinking. Loose parts give children the freedom to release their imagination and creativity. Rocks can become sculptures that morph and change at the children's desires. Colorful tiles can be arranged in complex and aesthetically pleasing patterns. Colorful bottles can be arranged to re-create the pattern of a rainbow and changed

again and combined with ribbon to fashion a variety of color combinations covered in the color wheel. Loose parts offer children many opportunities to engage in collaborative art. Building a large structure with boxes, crates, and spools allows children to negotiate and share their aesthetic values. Creating a mural using sticky notes and dots engages children in discussions and analysis of the work they are creating. Friedrich Froebel, the "father of kindergarten," acknowledged the importance for children to not only create their own art but also enjoy the art of others. He views the arts as the way children can reach their full potential (Froebel 2005).

Tomas and the Popsicle Sticks

Tomas is often seen creating art using loose parts. He can spend the day in the rock garden building sophisticated rock sculptures. Some days he works with other children to create tile murals. He has many suggestions about how to use art materials, and his aesthetic eye is impressive. On Monday Tomas arrives at the center and immediately notices the colorful craft sticks that have been added to the art center. He spends the morning testing different patterns and color combinations, guided by the color wheel that has been placed in the environment. He sorts the sticks by color and exclaims, "Look, there are many blues and many different greens!" He gets up and goes to get one of the many mirrors available in the environment. "I want to see how they 'refect' [reflect] in the mirror." He spends the rest of the morning testing many color combinations and surfaces, from mirrors to white felt and black felt. He compares and contrasts the different patterns he creates. He cuts the sticks and uses smaller pieces to create houses, figure people, and rainbows. At the end of the day, the craft sticks are arranged in a variety of complex patterns and art that take up a large area of the floor.

Space refers to the emptiness around or within objects. Frames combined with bottle caps, paint swatches, and tiles can give children the opportunity to explore the concept of space as they fill the entire frame or create specific designs utilizing only parts of the space provided by the frame. Ellen sprinkles a rainbow of colorful aquarium gravel inside the picture frame: first an arc of blue, then one of purple, red, orange, and pink. She drops green gravel off to the rainbow's side to be grass and not part of the rainbow.

Line is the path of a point moving through space. Children explore this concept as they arrange small white pebbles to create long and short lines. This helps them realize that a series of dots placed close together create lines. Annalisa uses black and white stones to create lines: a meandering line, lines that make the letter *I*, and lines on top of the picture frame's border.

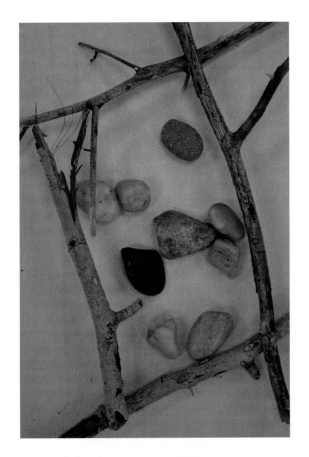

Form refers to three-dimensional geometric figures expressing width, length, and depth. Loose parts such as cardboard tubes, boxes, balls, and wooden dowels engage children to explore the concept of three-dimensional geometric shapes. Sarah uses pebbles and twigs to create a picture of herself walking on a rocky beach on a sunny day.

Shape implies spatial form and is usually perceived as two-dimensional. Loose parts can be arranged to create a multitude of geometric and organic shapes. Ribbon can be cut to equal sizes to create triangles. Acorns and seashells can be arranged as circles or squares. Bracelets and napkin rings give children the opportunity to explore circles. Alexis methodically fashions her vision of a horse with square mosaic tiles.

Pattern is a mark or design that suggests repetition and regularity in some recurring sequence. Patterns can be seen everywhere, from fabrics to brick pavers that form a pathway and to wooden planks of a deck. Megan's interest in flowers is seen as she makes a sunflower with a cinnamon stick stem, a lemon slice, and green leaves. She repeats the flower pattern three times.

CHAPTER 6

Design

Design is the creative process of interpreting something. It is a value judgment about a work of art. In art, the effectiveness of an artist's idea is revealed when the artistic elements—line, color, shape, texture, pattern, balance, space, mass, or volume—are arranged. Children use creativity as they experiment with artistic elements and express their visual ideas or designs. In our daily life, we experience the benefit of great design everywhere, and we may also begrudge poor design. Design is present in every aspect of our lives, from works of art to the signs on a highway, and to the buildings we live and work in.

Children use loose parts to design and redesign a wide variety of possibilities, from the simple to the intricate. When children use loose parts in designing, they gain a deeper understanding of how things are built or engineered and the functionality of the loose parts. Through loose parts, children make connections to how things work—their natural creativity and inventiveness blossom, and they acquire a keen sense for aesthetics.

The White Flower

Teacher Lisa places containers of glass stones, white rocks, sea glass, and glass tiles at a table for the children to use. When Annalisa, Jenna, and Sarah see the inviting materials, they immediately begin to create designs. Annalisa seems interested in making a flower design. She places a sky-blue glass stone on the placemat and then proceeds to set a circle of small white rocks around the glass stone. She carefully continues to make a long curved line of white rocks radiating from the design. The rock line appears to be the flower's stem. The placement of the stones reveals a successful expression of her flower design.

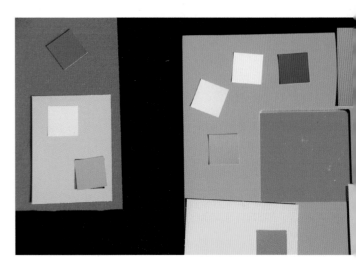

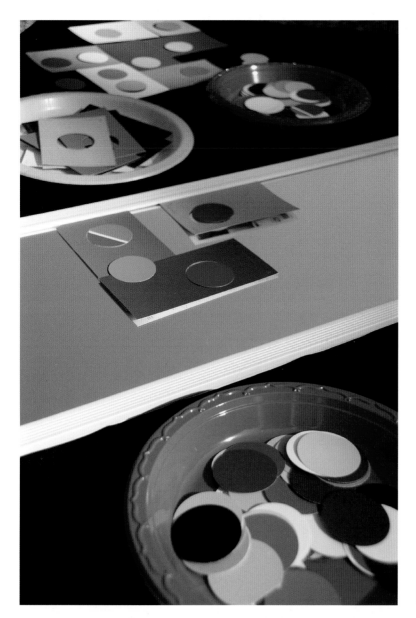

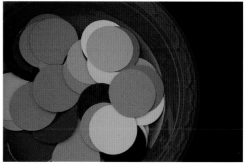

Jeannine, Conley, and Shane have been playing with the paint swatches that have squares cut from the middle. They keep changing the colors by interchanging the little squares inside the larger square. Their interest diminishes until circles are added into the environment. They begin to combine circles and squares into wonderful combinations. The small change of adding circles helps keep their interest while still maintaining consistency.

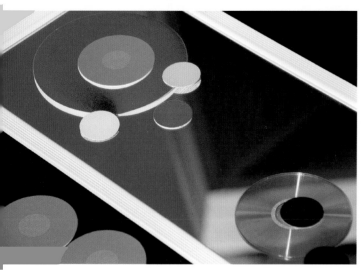

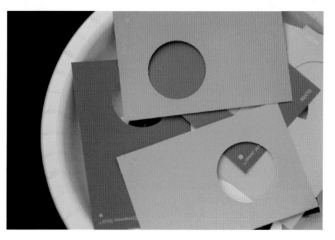

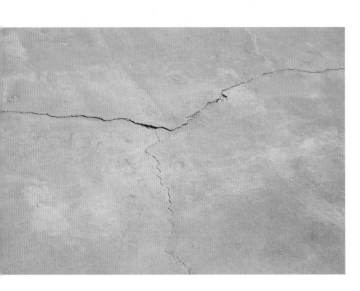

Unity focuses on bringing every element of design together, making certain that one element is not more important than the other. Shelton and Ariel spend time finding the perfect rocks to create a complex labyrinth on the sport court, using rocks similar in textures and size. They place each rock with precision along the cracks making sure that one rock is not more prominent than the other.

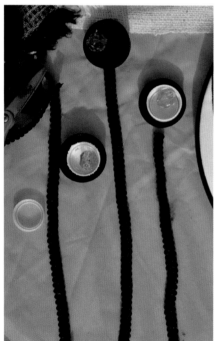

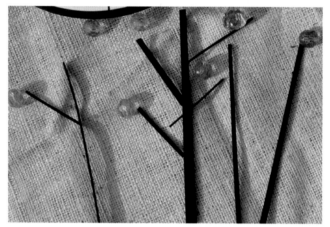

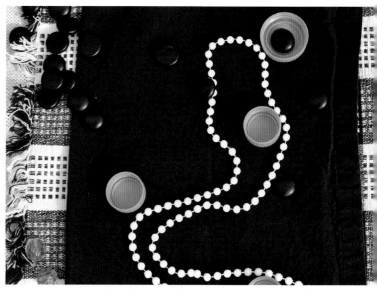

Emphasis is the part of the design that catches the viewer's attention. Emphasis is created by controlling color, proportion (scale and size), texture, and shapes, or by isolating specific elements. Trisha creates a complex design with gold beads and black stones. She drapes the gold beads on the fabric following the contour of the yellow-orange print of oval flowers. Suddenly she stops and places black stones on the flower stems. She is intentionally creating emphasis in her design.

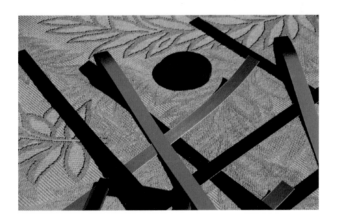

Movement is used to guide viewers to focal areas, often with lines, shapes, and colors. Alisia puts long strips of black paper in patterns on the fern rug. She starts by laying the strips in sections, making a grid. She then takes rubber cylinders and disks and places them inside the divided spaces. She has created a sense of movement and rhythm in her design.

Harmony refers to the combination of similar or related elements, such as adjacent colors in the color wheel or texture found in similar natural objects. Ashlee, Sara, Adison, and Max work with perseverance on an elaborate maze of pinecones, needles, stones, and logs. They create an intricate and harmonious design using natural materials that combines size and texture.

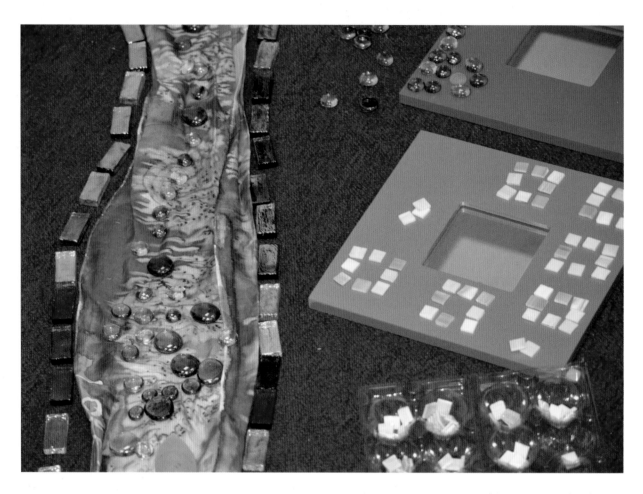

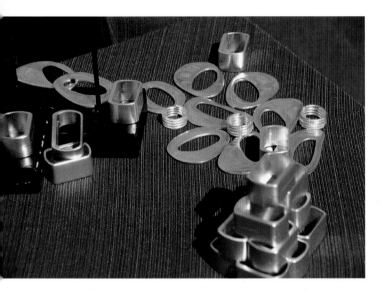

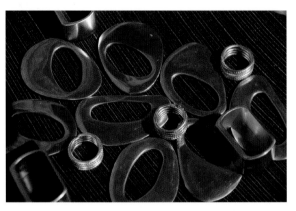

Proportion creates a sense of unity by bringing together all parts that relate well with each other, such as size, amount, and number of elements. Talisha works with metal cubes, cylinders, and rings to design a sculpture. The metal pieces appear to be in proportion to each other.

CHAPTER 7

Symbolic Play

Symbolic play allows children to fit the reality of the world into their own interests and knowledge. According to Piaget, symbolic play occurs when a child uses an object to represent or stand for another. Smilansky calls symbolic play dramatic play; Vygotsky labels it pretend play; and Pellegrini and Boyd refer to it as fantasy play (Sluss 2005). Symbolic play is significant, as it signifies the beginning of representational thought. It typically happens between the ages of two and seven. Children engage in symbolic play when they use a piece of bark as a car or baby bottle. They are using the bark to symbolize or represent the real objects. A mental image of a car and baby bottle and knowledge of the objects' functions are needed in order to use the bark as a substitute.

Loose parts are great materials to support each stage of symbolic play (the stages are defined on the following pages). A variety of small silk or plastic plants can be used to create a forest or a fairy garden. Fabric can help children build tents and forts to hide and reenact dramatic scenes. Scarves can be used to support hero play or create rivers in a farm scene where horses come to drink and rest. Tree cookies become stepping blocks for fairies and other little animals. Rocks become roads that lead to small towns built with twigs, wood rafts, and small wood tiles. When children pretend that a pebble is a little pet they can talk to, they are using symbols to think. They are increasing their cognitive abilities. When children work together to gather driftwood, shells, pebbles, and other natural loose parts, they learn to negotiate, gain control to make decisions, and gain social and emotional satisfaction.

Small worlds created with multiple loose parts give children the opportunity to claim a safe arena where they have power and control to express their thinking and test new rules. For example, children can create a fairy town using small mirrors to represent water, plastic plants to create gardens, and silk petals to represent blankets. In this small world, they use their imaginations to explore all the different things they imagine the fairies like, how they live, and what they do. The "play scripts" are a combination of children's real life experiences along with the fictional characters they are familiar with.

Our Own Town

An elaborate structure begins with Casey's idea to make a waterfall. She places a long blue silk scarf over large hollow blocks. The scarf cascades to the floor below. Katherine turns wooden blocks with transparent windows of colored plexiglass into a village. Aaron places a lantern in the middle of the town. It is a lighthouse to help the ships. At the waterfall's base a riverbed on a salmon-colored silk emerges with pinecones, acorns, and driftwood. Sam joins Casey to work diligently on creating an overpass with arches and roads running underneath. The small world turns into a larger world. The children join the play at various times and their imagination guides them to create new stories and characters. There are negotiations, arguments, and agreements. New rules are developed and changed as the play changes. Throughout this time the children have expressed their feelings and fears and found multiple ways to address them in their play. Strong relationships are formed and respect for each other is built as they represent and test their ideas.

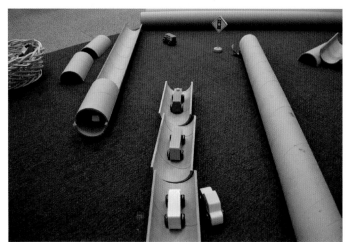

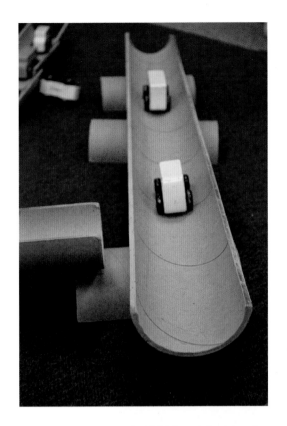

Stage one of symbolic play is imitation. Children begin symbolic play by imitating actions and words they have previously seen or heard, such as eating or sleeping (Johnson, Christie, and Wardle 2005). Teddy and Joey use cardboard carpet tubes and wooden blocks to re-create roads and bridges. They make engine noises of cars racing down the roadways and siren sounds of an ambulance crossing the bridge.

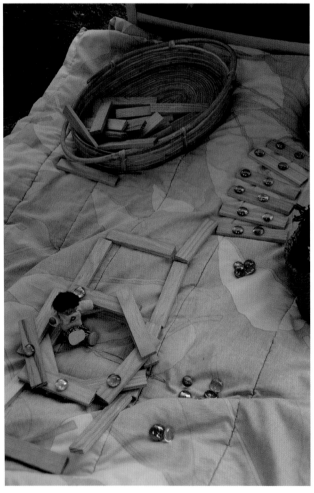

Children use sounds
in play (stage two).
Meredith makes gurgling
sounds as she pretends
the doll is near the river.
Later she can be heard
making clomping sounds
as she pretends to walk
the doll up the stairs.

Children use words in play (stage three). Elizabeth and Jakoby talk about how to arrange large hollow blocks to make a sofa. Elizabeth suggests they cover the sofa with a colorful fabric and comfy pillow to look like home. Next they discuss the addition of an outdoor garden for the little dolls to have dinner.

Stage four involves the make-believe use of objects. At this stage, children assign meaning to objects. For example, a green felt square becomes a pasture or blue glass stones become a river. Emilia covers the granny doll with acorns that serve as bubbles for granny's relaxing bubble bath.

In stage five, children begin the functional use of symbolic toys. Children use loose parts to imitate reality for the function that the object was intended. For instance, a turkey baster is used to suck up and squeeze out water. A scarf is used to wrap around one's neck. Ariel and Max set up a wide collection of tree cookies, tree blocks, silk plants, and a mirror to make a watering hole for the jungle animals.

Part 4
Action

Action alone is not sufficient for learning.

To understand their immediate world, children

must interact *thoughtfully* with it.

MARY HOHMANN AND DAVID P. WEIKART

Connecting/Disconnecting

Movement

Transporting

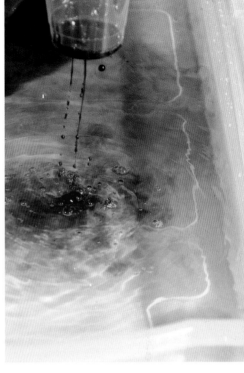

Through action, children learn about how people and objects move and what power they have to affect these movements.

When observing children playing, it is apparent that they engage in repetitive schemas or patterns. These schemas can best be defined as repetitive patterns of the same action that a child can apply to a variety of situations. These patterns are the result of the natural, uncontrollable urges children have to do something. These urges serve as a strong motivation and determination to accomplish what they have in mind. Schemas help children gain understanding of how things work. Schemas serve as building blocks and structures for learning and thinking. These repetitive behaviors forge important connections in the brain and establish play patterns that unfold as children make new discoveries and test new ideas. When children repeat the same action, they deepen their knowledge of how objects function. Through this repetitive and thoughtful play, children apply existing knowledge to new experiences. This helps them gain control over the world they live in (Athey 2007).

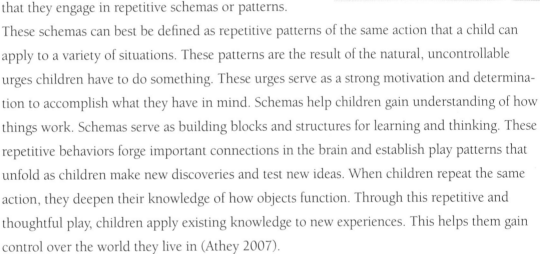

Most schemas demonstrate children's interest in movement or action. Loose parts support children's urges to provoke action and encourage them to explore objects in ingenious and creative ways. Setting gutters in the environment can encourage children to study the speed and trajectory of objects being dropped. Pendulums can help them understand how a rotating movement can knock over cardboard tubes placed around it. Fabric can help them create enclosures to hide and envelop themselves. Pipes, clothespins, and a variety of paper clips give children the opportunity to connect and disconnect objects. Loose parts can be transformed into what the children's imaginations determine. A large spool can become a fairy house. A group of branches can be the foundation for a building or part of a forest. A variety of plastic plants can become part of a swamp in the sandbox.

CHAPTER 8

Movement

We live in a world that is in constant motion. We are surrounded by both living and nonliving things, which move in different and often unpredictable ways. Movement is dependent on the forces applied to make an object change direction, stop, speed up, or slow down. Knowing how things move is important since it allows us to manipulate the forces that trigger movement. When we know how things move, we can predict what causes the movement and what we can do to control it. When we control the way things move, we restore a sense of order to chaos that is caused by

unpredictable and random movement. Children constantly explore how things move. They push balls to see if they move away or remain static. They exert different forces to change the direction of a spool, or they change the incline of a ramp to make a ball land in a different spot.

Children are active and in constant motion. They enjoy watching cardboard tubes, spools, balls, marbles, and other loose parts move, and they enjoy moving themselves. Loose parts are ideal to engage children in gaining a deeper understanding of how things and their bodies move.

Hula hoops can be used to learn about gliding or creating a circular motion. Tubes can be rolled down a ramp or an incline in the outdoor environment. Children learn to use their bodies to exert force to make a pulley or pendulum move to knock over items. Designing and building ramps with wooden planks and milk crates gives children the opportunity to test concepts such as gravity, motion, and cause and effect.

Why Do Things Fall? Because We Throw Them

Trish and Dave enjoy dropping balls, marbles, and other objects to see how they fall. They spend a lot of time testing which types of objects fall faster or slower. This leads to conversations during group meeting time. "What makes things fall?" asks Jenny. Dave, who is an eager scientist, is quick to answer, "They fall when we throw them." Trish says, "They still fall when we don't throw them."

To help them in their inquiry, cove molding and gutters are incorporated into the environment. There are also multiple loose parts to explore, including corks, Ping-Pong balls, marbles, and small spools. A stepladder is added to provide children with the opportunity to drop objects from higher heights. Tanya and Alexis join Trish and Dave in the investigation. All four children spend time dropping a variety of loose parts from various heights. With some help they start a chart to track the height objects are dropped from and how long it takes each object to fall. The children offer a variety of hypotheses. The teachers bring a chronometer to measure how long it takes each object to fall. Tanya, Alexis, Trish, and Dave take turns starting and stopping the chronometer. After many trials, they determine that the heavier objects, such as tree cookies and rocks, fall faster, while lighter objects, such as corks, feathers, and paint cards, fall slower. The children's ideas are recorded, and every day new loose parts are added to the area for children to use as they test their hypotheses.

After reading a book about gravity, Dave grabs a magnet wand and a handful of magnet balls. He places the wand on the floor and drops the magnet balls. Other children watch in fascination as some objects stick to the wand and others just roll away. Trish exclaims in excitement, "I get it, the magnet makes the thing fall!" Dave points to a page in the book and says, "No, the balls fall by gravity, not because the magnets make them fall."

Trajectory is the exploration of how objects move vertically, horizontally, across, up and down, and especially through the air. Children who follow a trajectory schema will throw balls up in the air, drop items from high places, use a hose to propel balls down a creek or small incline, squirt and splash water from a hose, or enjoy swinging.

Projectile movement is defined as any object that when dropped or thrown continues in motion through its own inaction and is only influenced by the pull of gravity. Aaron and Janelle roll hula hoops down the hill and watch to see which hoop makes it to the bottom first. Shan picks up a hula hoop, joins the play, and exclaims, "Let's race!" The children say together, "On your marks, *go!*" and release the hula hoops at the same time.

Rotation or *circulation* refers to how an object moves in a circular motion on its axis or point of rotation. Children enjoy spinning to the point of dizziness, they get engrossed with how wheels turn, and they spend time exploring how to create a circular motion with suspended items such as pendulums. Diego and Julian align small branch stumps in a circle around the pendulum. Diego holds the ball at the end of the pendulum, counting, "One, two, three." He releases the ball and only half of the branch stumps fall down. Julian says, "Let's try again, but this time we have to make sure the pendulum knocks them all out."

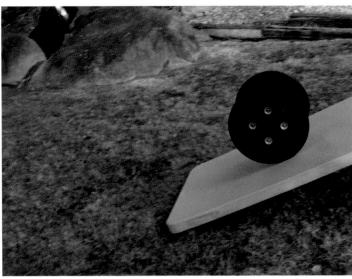

MOVEMENT **123**

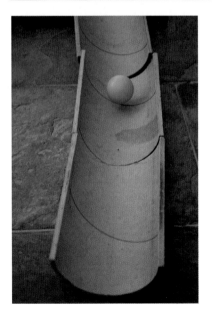

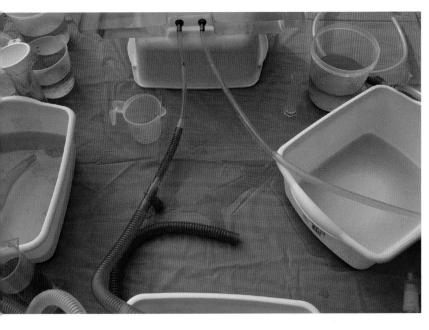

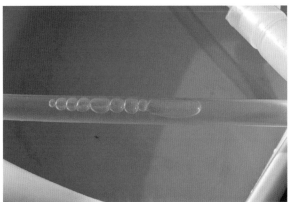

Gliding refers to moments when objects or people move in a smooth and continuous motion. Children explore how to roll balls or other items on smooth surfaces. Water walls can help children understand the concept of gliding or moving smoothly over a slick surface. They also enjoy pushing colorful bottle caps and moving them on top of a mirror or smooth surface. Oliver pours water in the water wall and watches carefully as the water slides from the top to the bottom. He exclaims, "Look, the water goes smooth in the white part" (referring to a gutter).

CHAPTER 9

Transporting

Children spend time picking up objects and transporting them around the yard or classroom. They enjoy filling up baskets with pebbles or beads and then dumping them. Children use buckets to gather sand and dirt and move them from one end of the sandbox to the other. They may also transport heftier items such as branches, bricks, logs, and rocks. They fill up wagons, strollers, and carts with pipes, containers, and boxes. Transporting schema involves mathematical and language concepts. When children collect objects and move them using bags or baskets, it helps them learn the concepts of weight and space. They also begin to predict how many objects they can add to the bag. They discuss how many objects they can carry before the bag is too heavy.

To support children's interest in transporting, environments should include a variety of sizes and types of bags, baskets, buckets, boxes, containers, bottles, and cans. Fabric in various sizes can also be used to encompass bundles and create stretchers. Fabric and scarves can be stuffed into pillowcases for children to fill and empty. Taking baskets and buckets on walks provides a place for children to collect treasures.

When pulleys and zip lines are used with buckets or baskets, they help children move items up and down or across large areas. Including large and small tubes, watering cans, and hoses can help children transport water into the sandbox or the garden. Envelopes and small boxes can serve to hold and transport treasures found in the classroom or on walks.

We Did It, We Are Strong

Colton loves moving loose parts both outdoors and indoors. He is very skilled at figuring out how to move large and heavy objects. On this particular day, a group of children are building a structure using branches, fabric, and rope. Colton discovers a large branch at the end of the yard and wants to move it to the area where the structure is being built. He tries to lift it and realizes it is too heavy. He calls to Samantha and Dave: "Hey, bring fabric and come help me." The children lay the fabric on the ground, and they work together to drag the branch on top of the fabric. Once the branch is on top, they pull the fabric to the area where they are building. Colton exclaims, "We did it! We are stronger than the branch!"

As they finish the structure, the children decide they want to line it with rocks. They get a large bucket and start filling it with rocks. They try to lift it, but it is too heavy. Dave says, "Let's get a wheelbarrow." They fill the wheelbarrow and take turns pushing it to the construction area. In the meantime, Samantha wants to line the area with some of the leaves on the ground. She gets a basket and fills it with leaves and transports them to the structure. She dumps the leaves on the ground and counts them as she covers the area. She says, "Look, I used three and five [meaning 35] leaves to cover the space." This intentional work continues and the children move multiple items into the structure.

Large and small containers that can be filled with acorns, buckeyes, pebbles, gravel, leaves, and twigs allow children to understand volume. "How many buckeyes can I fit in the basket? One, two, three. I think it has space for five," says Dante while transporting them around the classroom.

When children transport, they can determine the accessibility of the items they want to move. They learn the concepts of more and less and enough or not enough. Cans on low shelves are easily accessible and encourage children to transport a variety of loose parts. Loose parts can be added to the cans to provoke children's interests.

Children learn the concepts of empty and full when they fill, transport, and dump. Samantha is filling a bucket with rocks. As she works she says, "Now this bucket is full and the others are empty."

Children test how portable items are and the best way to move them. They learn that it may be easier to move leaves than it is to move pebbles. They also realize that even when leaves are lighter than pebbles, they may need a larger container to move them. Sophie is moving sycamore pods using a metal container. As she walks, the pods keep falling out of the container. After a few attempts, Sophie says, "I need a bigger container so that the pods fit better and don't fall."

When children move objects, they learn about weight. They compare and contrast the size and weight of an object, and they estimate what type of container they need to move the item. "I need a strong container to move these bottles; the bags keep breaking!" exclaims Sean as he moves them from one end of the playground to the area where he is building a castle.

CHAPTER 10

Connecting/ Disconnecting

When educators carefully observe children playing, they see how children enjoy spending time connecting and disconnecting objects. Children use tape to join papers together, and they place and replace sticky notes to create different designs. Velcro rollers can be connected and disconnected easily, and they can also be attached to different surfaces. Children can create designs on felt boards, or they can build tall pyramids and complex structures.

When children spend time connecting and disconnecting objects, they are developing problem-solving skills and coming up with creative solutions to attach items together. They work to figure out the properties of each object and how to connect them. Masking tape is stickier than transparent tape and may link items with more ease. They realize that magnets have opposing forces and they figure out ways to use them to connect train cars. They explore a variety of clips to connect and hang scarves and ribbon in the environment. In the process they learn that some clips are easier to manipulate with their fingers, but they may not hold heavy items as well as bigger clips.

Loose parts support children's interests in connecting and disconnecting. They help them understand how things work and eventually make connections to guide their ideas, such as attaching individual parts to make a whole.

The Pipe Aqueduct

Jack, Samantha, and Colton are digging in the sandbox. "We need water," Jack says as he picks up a pipe and connects it to a longer pipe. Colton looks up and tells Jack, "It is not long enough to get water." Samantha and Jack go over to the container full of pipes and carry four large pipes back to the sandbox. They connect the four pipes to the previous two. They lay the pipes down toward the water hose and extend the hose to reach the pipes. Colton says, "We still need more pipes." Samantha gets another pipe and asks, "How many?" "I think one," answers Jack. They use the last pipe Samantha brought. "No, no, it's too long," says Colton. They take the pipe off and look for a shorter pipe to use. Finally, they connect the pipes to the hose on the water wall and run back to the sandbox. "Yeah, we have water!" Colton screams in excitement as Samantha and Jack start shoveling sand over the water.

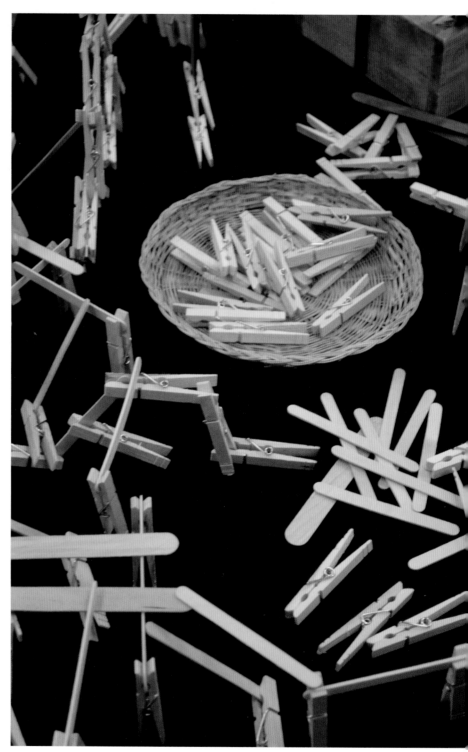

When children explore loose parts, they gain knowledge about the properties of each object. Clothespins and craft sticks can be connected to build structures and imaginary play spaces. Serina enjoys connecting clothespins. Indoors she uses them to create structures by connecting them to craft sticks. After a rainy day, we go outside and Serina begins to pick wet leaves. She uses the clothespins to connect the leaves to the loom and says, "I am lining all these leaves to dry, and then we can take them inside."

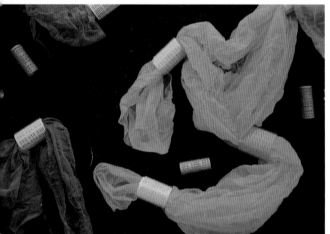

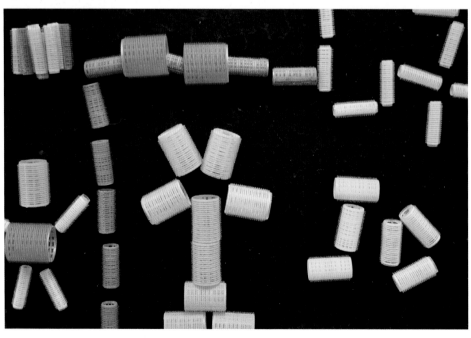

When children work to connect loose parts, they learn about the association between cause and effect. When hangers are placed together and they stay connected or fall, children learn that their strategy has worked or failed. Children also develop spatial relationship knowledge as they connect and line loose parts together. Tommy and Adriana notice the basket of hangers by the tree. Tommy says, "Let's make a mobile." Adriana and Tommy connect the hangers, finding the perfect balance. They add ribbons and CDs to the mobile throughout the week. The mobile becomes a lovely work of art and adds beauty to the outdoor environment.

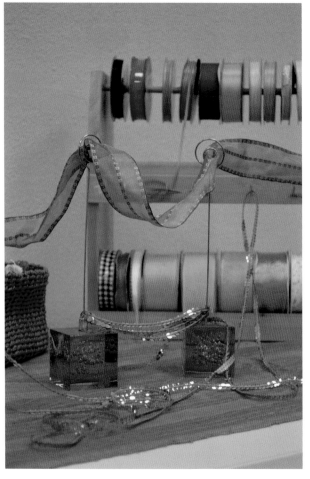

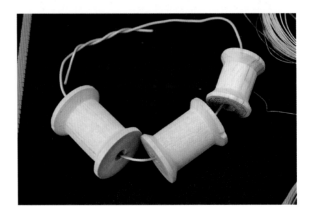

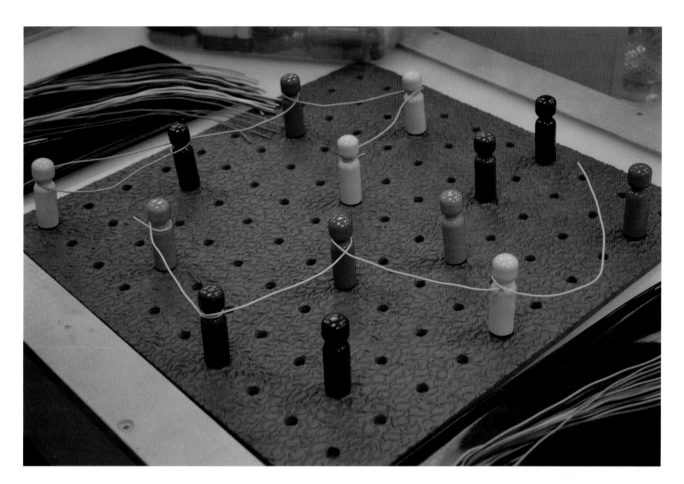

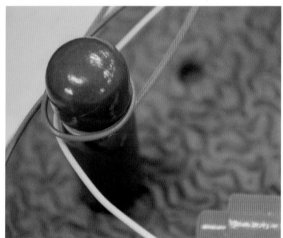

Children use loose parts to explore how items interact together; for example, they learn that in order for things to stick together, they need to be tied or connected with a sticky substance. When they connect wooden pegs with colorful wire, they understand how items and colors go together. In this process, they integrate new knowledge into their current understanding of how items work and function. Aaron is intently wrapping wire around colorful pegs. He takes the wire off the pegs and exclaims, "Look, the wire is now shaped by the pegs; I made many loops!"

Part 5
Inquiry

If a child is to keep alive his inborn sense of wonder, he needs the companionship of at least one adult who can share it, rediscovering with him the joy, excitement, and mystery of the world we live in.

RACHEL CARSON

Construction

Investigation

Correlation

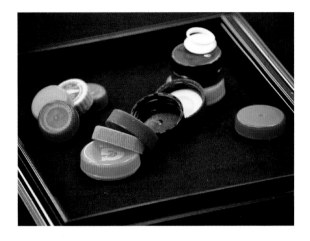
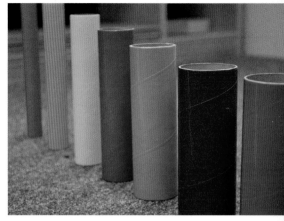

Inquiry is seeking knowledge through questions—it is both a practical and cognitive activity.

Children's curiosity moves them to explore and ask many questions that lead to in-depth explorations of immediate interest to them. Children are innately curious beings. From birth, they demonstrate an instinct for inquiry and a strong sense of wonder that motivates them to learn about their environment. Their desire to question, hypothesize, explore, and investigate is an inherent part of who they are. Loose parts support the curiosity and inquisitive nature of young children.

Young children ask many questions to make sense of their world and their place in it. Their curiosity and natural sense of wonder drive them to explore and investigate the answers to their questions. In doing this they are in control of their own learning, which encourages their spirit to explore and investigate what interests them. Loose parts are invitations for learning; they provoke curiosity and excite children to explore and investigate their multiple uses. Children can redesign, repurpose, and incorporate loose parts into long-term inquiry-based investigations. Loose parts are "intelligent" materials that stimulate the scientist qualities in every child.

An important component of inquiry is imagination. Children have an unconventional way of looking at patterns that may not be obvious to adults. They are creative when they look for answers. In order to develop their sense of wonder, children need the freedom to be physically involved with the environment. Children's curiosity grows when provocations that invoke discovery, exploration, asking questions, testing theories, making plans, and thinking deeply are included in the environment. A variety of loose parts support children's inquiry and imagination and interest in lifelong learning.

CHAPTER 11

Construction

Children are interested in building and testing their theories about the functioning of the physical and social world in which they live. They are just as interested in building as they are in demolishing and dissecting the structures they build. Building and constructing allow children to translate abstract images in their mind or imagination and creatively turn these images into concrete objects. It helps them foster problem-solving skills and develop divergent thinking. Loose parts engage children in constructive play. They can build a tent or a fort using branches and a variety of fabrics. They can design a town using sticks, pebbles, and rocks. They can create a dam using branches and twigs or a large structure using cardboard boxes. They can test their engineering skills by using gutters to construct an aqueduct to transport water. Loose parts help develop future engineers, architects, scientists, artists, designers, and mathematicians. The possibilities are limited only by the variety and number of loose parts included in the environment.

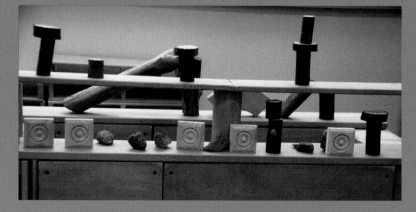

Can We Make Things Fit?

Amanda, Leah, and Sean are creating a large enclosure using branches, large spools, fabric, and string. They want to make the enclosure big enough for the three of them to fit inside. They are planning to create a quiet space with pillows and blankets for reading and resting. They start by sharing their ideas with each other. They draw plans and gather the materials they need. As they work together, they run into a few challenges. First, they realize that the fabric is too heavy and its weight makes the structure collapse. Amanda takes a few steps back and says, "Oh no, we need to get more branches so it stays up." They take a few more branches, and with adult help they are able to create the structure. They tie string on top of the branches to secure them. They place the fabric on top of the structure, and this time it stays. The children clap in excitement and run to get pillows and blankets. When the three of them try to get in, they run into another challenge. Sean says, "Uh-oh, we don't fit. What are we going to do?" This leads into finding other ways to add space. They drape fabric on top of a branch to create a shady and quiet space to play, and they secure the ends to the ground using rocks. The children use this quiet space for a few days to read and get away from the excitement of the classroom.

Spatial awareness in children is the way they learn how items or objects are positioned in space in relationship to their own bodies. It is the way they navigate the world and manipulate the space around them. Spatial awareness helps children design a building and engineer a solid structure. From an understanding of spatial awareness, children begin to learn other concepts, such as direction, location, and distance. After unpacking some supplies, boxes are placed in the outdoor space for children to explore. Antoine and Tamika begin to pile up the boxes. Antoine invites others; Jillian joins and excitedly says, "We can build high and long to the side so we can all fit."

Mathematical thinking occurs when children build and construct; they develop their logical-mathematical knowledge. They spend time comparing and contrasting the attributes of the different objects they use in building. They become aware of patterns and sequences and how these patterns help them design their structures. Ceci and Sebastian build a castle with Kapla blocks and tree cookies. Ceci says, "Look, we can use the pebbles to decorate the castle." Sebastian responds, "Yes, we can line them up one next to the other." Ceci says in excitement, "Here's the tower" as she places a gourd on top of a tree cookie structure.

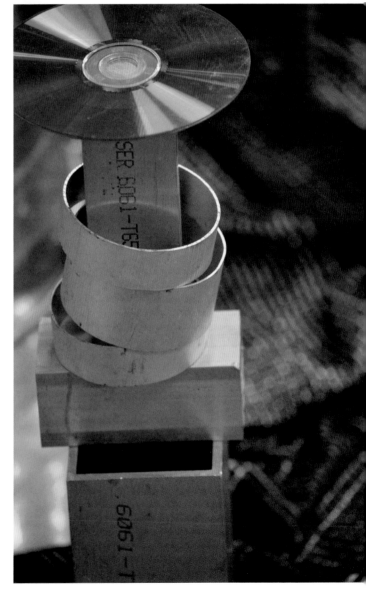

Children are natural scientists, and when they engage in building, they experiment and develop complex hypotheses. They test their hypotheses, such as "How can rolls of paper be supported in construction?" As they build they learn important scientific concepts such as gravity and cause and effect. Danita says, "Let's make a sculpture like this," pointing to a photography book of sculptures intentionally left in the block area. They attempt to balance the paper rolls together, but the rolls fall. Joseph gets a colorful box and places it in the middle of the block area and exclaims, "Here, they'll balance now!"

CHAPTER 12

Investigation

The process of investigation is an innate part of human behavior. Infants utilize all their senses to explore and collect information that helps them make meaning of their world. When toddlers drop an object repeatedly, they are investigating what happens to it. Will the object come back or will it stay down? When children engage in investigations, they are involved in asking probing questions,

collecting data, analyzing the information, and finding meaningful answers to their original questions. This reflective process helps them make connections and understand the connections between previous knowledge and new experiences and ideas. John Dewey argues that children must think to learn and that in-depth investigation supports reflection and inquiry (Dewey 1933).

Loose parts offer children multiple opportunities to investigate their ideas. A scale surrounded by pinecones, rocks, a variety of plastic parts, and metal washers helps children generate hypotheses of which item weighs more. Tree stumps and two-by-four planks allow children to create pathways and ramps to test balance and how their bodies move in relationship to the stumps. Tiles give children the opportunity to investigate color as they design complex patterns. In other words, loose parts are perfect for investigating and learning.

Balance, Balance, and More Balance

The children's interest in balance started when they watched each other walk a complex pathway they created using tree stumps and wood planks. They experimented walking with their hands to the front and their hands to their sides. They noticed how extending their hands to their sides was helpful in maintaining their balance. This interest in balance was carried on to the tree cookies. They spent time attempting to balance tree cookies with a rock in between each cookie. They discussed how centering the cookies in the middle provided balance. After a few days, they began to experiment with cardboard tubes of various sizes. That presented an entire new set of challenges. The children finally decided that the reason they could not balance the tubes on top of each other was because they needed a broader rectangular base. This moved them to combine the boxes available in the environment with the tubes. Now they also want to see how high they can build and still maintain balance. The structure is exciting, and many of the children and the adults join in. A stepladder is brought out, and a ten-foot tower is built. Sean exclaims in excitement, "Now I know that to balance we need a rectangle!"

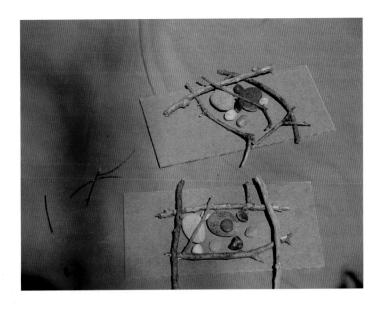

Being able to make a comparison provides understanding between the parts of a whole. When children take an item and compare it to another item, they gain knowledge of how things work— how they are the same and how they are different. Sean sorts shells by size. He takes a magnifying glass and carefully examines the different shells. After a few minutes, he says, "They are different sizes, but they look the same. They have some different colors too." He gets very quiet, and after a moment he says, "That makes each shell special."

The concepts of physics are explored as children learn about the nature and properties of matter and energy, including mechanics, heat, light, sound, gravity, refraction, and magnetism. Children can learn about refraction by playing with prisms, opaque and transparent loose parts on the light table, and an overhead projector. Tina places some transparent pieces on the overhead projector and says, "You can only see the lines outside and not the center." She places a series of colored acrylic cylinders on the projector's glass and points to the image projected on the wall, saying, "Now you can see the middle because it has color."

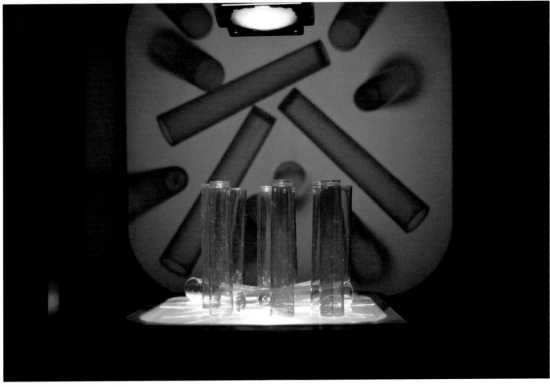

Through science, children generate hypotheses, ask questions, test ideas, and find multiple solutions to a problem. This facilitates gaining a deeper knowledge about the natural and physical world. Trevor hypothesizes about what weighs more: pinecones or driftwood. He places several small pinecones on one weighing platform of a large-sized scale and a piece of driftwood on the other weighing platform. Trevor says, "I thought the pinecones would weigh more than the driftwood because there are lots of pinecones, but they weigh the same."

When children learn from their natural world, they gain empathy and the ability to nurture living things. As they discover the wonders of nature, they gain a reverence for life. Natural materials such as tree cookies, olives, and pebbles engage Aria's interest. She spends time moving and arranging them to create small sculptures. She investigates each acorn and sorts them by size. She compares the different pebbles and arranges them in lines and circles. She makes faces using cinnamon sticks as hair, acorns as eyes, and a tree cookie as a mouth. She picks up the cinnamon sticks, smells them, and says, "This smells sweet."

CHAPTER 13

Correlation

In nature and the physical world, most objects have some kind of relationship to one another. When we know the value of one variable in an object, we can predict the value of other variables within the object. For instance, when children engage in loose parts play, they can find correlations between how fast a Ping-Pong ball will roll down a ramp and the incline of the ramp. Children can collect data and analyze the correlation between the positioning of the ramp to the speed the Ping-Pong ball moves. They can analyze the data and make concise plans to accomplish the goal of making the balls go slow or fast. The purpose of correlation is to reduce the range of uncertainty and bring it close to reality. Since correlation is positive when the values increase together and are negative when one value decreases and the other increases, children know that the higher the incline, the faster the ball will move. This helps children gain a deeper understanding that in nature and the physical world there are multiplicities of interrelated forces.

Playing with a wide variety of loose parts is an interactive way for children to acquire fundamental mathematical concepts such as classification, measurement, one-to-one

correspondence, and seriation. Children naturally sort and classify rocks, pebbles, tiles, and pinecones. They line up loose parts to measure. For instance, a child may line bottle caps along a stick to get an idea of the stick's length. Children work on one-to-one correspondence by placing buttons in the cups of an egg carton. They learn about seriation by arranging wooden spoons by size. The possibilities for learning are endless.

How Big Is the Tree's Shadow?

On a walk around the school's orchard, the children notice the shadow a tall tree is casting. They immediately start to guess how tall the tree is based on the shadow. The children walk around the tree and touch the bark.

David says, "That is a big tree."

"The tree shadow is bigger," shares Sam.

Teacher Kelly says, "Tell me how you know that the shadow is bigger."

"Look, it is just long, that is how you know," answers Melody.

As they try to wrap their arms around the tree, Davis exclaims, "No, the tree is bigger. We can't hug it!"

The children notice the many pinecones, and they begin to pick them up and align them on top of the tree's shadow. They count the pinecones as they place them, "One, two, three. . . ." After they are done placing the pinecones, they begin to gather tree branches and line them up next to the pinecones. Then they move on to placing rocks. This hard work goes on for a while. The children begin to chart on paper how many items they line up next to the tree. They estimate the size of the tree based on the number of items placed by the shadow. The children realize that the shadow is as long as the length of twenty pinecones, ten branches, and fifteen rocks. Armed with this information, they return to their classroom ready to use measuring tapes to assess the height of the tree.

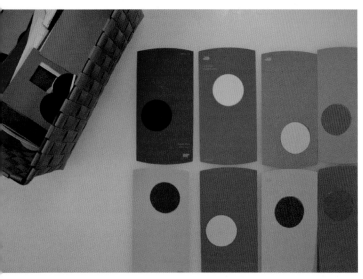

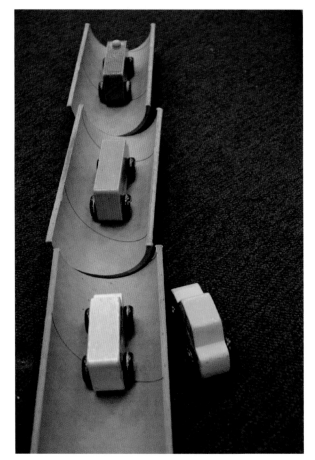

One-to-one correspondence is the understanding that one group has as many objects as another. Before children can count, they need to be able to understand the concept of one-to-one correspondence. As Elisabeth places one pinecone in each muffin tin cup, she demonstrates an understanding that one pinecone matches one muffin tin cup.

Classification is the ability to group or sort items into sets based on specific characteristics, such as size, color, shape, weight, or height. Children can classify felt balls by color and size. They can arrange craft sticks and pipe cleaners by length. They can sort beach glass by transparency and opacity. With practice, children learn that things belong together because of what they do—in other words, by the purpose of each item. Shanne exclaims in excitement, "Look, I have a tiny pink felt ball, medium balls, and a large ball. I have all pinks together!"

Geometry is the ability to work with points, lines, shapes, and space. It begins with visual understanding. Children recognize shapes and judge them by appearance of the whole instead of distinguishing individual parts of a shape. They can create shapes using twigs, sticks, pebbles, rocks, and pipes. Erika arranges two triangles together on the light table. "Look, when I put triangles together, I get a square!"

Comparison is the ability to distinguish differences and similarities in objects. For instance, children can compare items based on size, color, or functionality. Tomas is comparing various ways to write his name. He re-creates the letters in his name by using hair rollers on a felt board and metal brackets on an oil drip pan. He points to each letter. "It says Tomas, T-O-M-A-S."

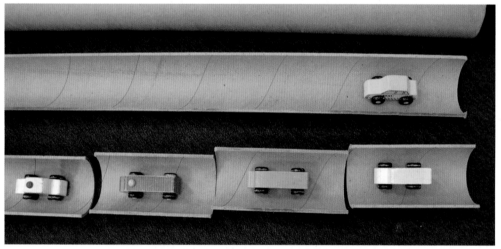

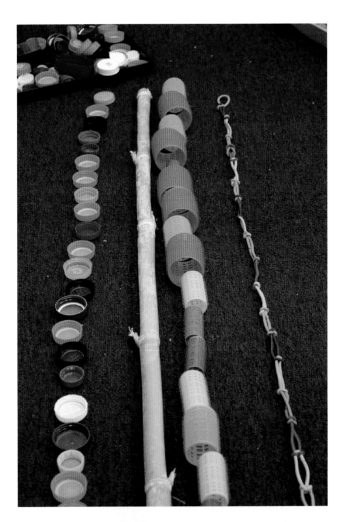

Ways to measure are explored as children discover length, height, and weight of objects. Understanding the concepts of measurement begins with analyzing the attributes of a variety of objects. Teacher Lisa asks Sam and Teddy if it will take more caps or hair rollers to make a line as long as the bamboo pole. "Let's find out," Sam says eagerly as he places plastic caps side by side along the bamboo pole while Teddy places hair rollers end to end. "Hey, it takes more caps than rollers to make it as long as the pole," Teddy exclaims. Teacher Lisa inquires, "What about rubber bands?" Sam shouts, "That's going to take a lot. Come on, Teddy."

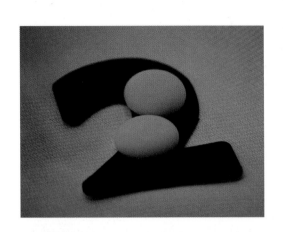

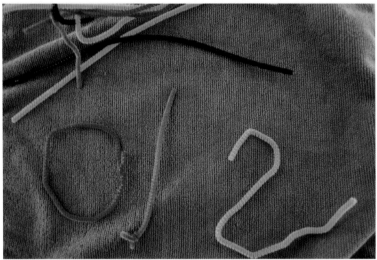

Counting and numbers are part of young children's everyday lives. It starts with a simple intuition and develops into the ability to use and understand the relative values of numbers. Children enjoy counting collections of rocks, shells, colorful rubber bands, and small and large tree stumps. William places the numerals 8, 6, 5, 3, and 2 above a plastic sorting container. He works on dropping tile pieces in each compartment to match the corresponding numeral above. "See, Teacher Miriam, the fives go here and the threes go here. It's going to take a lot to do eight."

Patterning is a mathematical concept that involves making visual, auditory, or motor regularities, such as placing items in a sequence by color or size. As Kara explores the sea glass, she puts pieces in an A-A-B-A-A-B pattern. She comments to herself, "It goes like this: blue, blue, brown; blue, blue, brown."

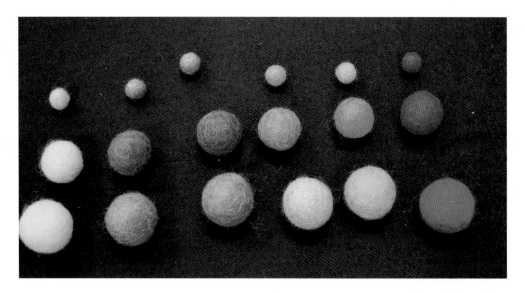

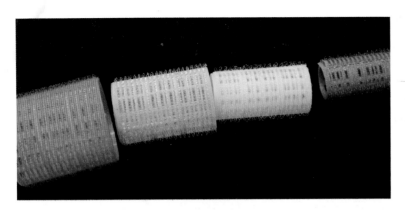

Seriation is the ability to arrange or position objects based on differences and gradual variations in their qualities. For example, children can order items by size, width, length, or height. Liana skillfully nests the colored cardboard tubes so that each one fits into the larger ones. Next, she works persistently over several days to arrange the tubes by height. At first she places the tallest and smallest tubes at opposite ends, but the middle tubes are randomly arranged. She looks puzzled at their placement. Eventually she successfully orders the tubes by height.

References

Armitage, Marc. 2009. *Play Pods in Schools: An Independent Evaluation (2006–2009)*. United Kingdom: Playpeople.

Asbury, Carolyn, and Barbara Rich, eds. 2008. *Learning, Arts, and the Brain*. New York: Dana Press.

Athey, Chris. 2007. *Extending Thought in Young Children: A Parent-Teacher Partnership*. 2nd ed. London: Paul Chapman Publishing.

Bagley, Donna M., and Patricia H. Klass. 1997. "Comparison of the Quality of Preschoolers' Play in Housekeeping and Thematic Sociodramatic Play Centers." *Journal of Research in Childhood Education* 12 (1): 71–77.

Bohling, Vicki, Cindy Saarela, and Dana Miller. 2010. *This Never Would Have Happened Indoors: Supporting Preschool-Age Children's Learning in Nature Explore Classroom in Minnesota*. Lincoln, NE: Dimensions Educational Research Foundation. www.dimensionsfoundation.org/research /documents/skillsforestlkmn_10.pdf.

Bretherton, Inge. 1998. "Reality and Fantasy in Make-Believe Play." In *Readings from Play as a Medium for Learning and Development,* ed. Doris Bergen, 67–69. Olney, MD: Association for Childhood Education International.

Brown, Stuart. 2009. *Play: How It Shapes the Brain, Opens the Imagination, and Invigorates the Soul*. With Christopher Vaughan. New York: Avery.

Collard, Paul. 2012. "What Is a Creative Education and Why Is It Important?" Keynote speech presented at the Scottish Learning Festival. Glasgow, September 20. www.educationscotland .gov.uk/video/s/video_tcm4732792.asp?strReferringChannel=slf&strReferringPageID=tcm :4-714396-64&class=l1+d150071.

Copple, Carol, and Sue Bredekamp, eds. 2009. *Developmentally Appropriate Practice in Early Childhood Programs: Serving Children from Birth through Age 8*. 3rd ed. Washington, DC: National Association for the Education of Young Children.

Dempsey, Jim, and Eric Strickland. 1993. "The 'Whys' Have It! Why to Include Loose Parts on the Playground," adapted from *A Right to Play: Proceedings of the American Association for the Child's Right to Play*, eds. Marcy Guddemi and Tom Jambor. Little Rock, Arkansas: Southern

Early Childhood Association. http://www.scholastic.com/teachers/article/staff-workshop-teacher-handout-quotwhysquot-have-it-why-include-loose-parts-playground-0.

Dewey, John. 1933. *How We Think: A Restatement of the Relation of Reflective Thinking to the Educative Process.* Boston: D. C. Heath and Company.

———. 1990. *The School and Society and the Child and the Curriculum.* Chicago: The University of Chicago Press.

Dodge, Mary K., and Joe L. Frost. 1986. "Children's Dramatic Play: Influence of Thematic and Nonthematic Settings." *Childhood Education* 62 (3): 166–70.

Edwards, Linda Carol, Kathleen M. Bayless, and Marjorie E. Ramsey. 2009. *Music and Movement: A Way of Life for the Young Child.* 6th ed. Upper Saddle River, NJ: Merrill.

Fisch, Karl, and Scott McLeod. 2012. "Did You Know? Shift Happens." YouTube video, 4:58. Posted February 28 by "VideoShredHead." www.youtube.com/watch?v=YmwwrGV_aiE.

Fox, Jill Englebright, and Robert Schirrmacher. 2012. *Art & Creative Development for Young Children.* 7th ed. Belmont, CA: Wadsworth.

Froebel, Friedrich. 2005. *The Education of Man.* Translated by W. N. Hailmann. New York: Dover Publications, Inc. First published 1826.

Gleave, Josie. 2008. *Risk and Play: A Literature Review.* London: National Children's Bureau. www.playday.org.uk/media/2661/risk_and_play___a_literature_review.pdf.

Guilford, J. P. 1967. "Creativity Research: Past, Present and Future." In *Frontiers of Creativity Research: Beyond the Basics*, ed. Scott G. Isaksen, 33–65. Buffalo, NY: Bearly Limited.

Hewes, Jane. 2006. *Let the Children Play: Nature's Answer to Early Learning.* Montreal, Quebec: Early Childhood Learning Knowledge Centre.

Johnson, James E., James F. Christie, and Francis Wardle. 2005. *Play, Development, and Early Education.* Boston: Pearson.

Kamii, Constance, and Rheta DeVries. 1993. *Physical Knowledge in Preschool Education: Implications of Piaget's Theory.* New York: Teachers College Press.

Kuczaj, Stan A. 1985. "Language Play." *Early Child Development and Care* 19 (1–2): 53–67.

Louv, Richard. 2008. *Last Child in the Woods: Saving Our Children from Nature-Deficit Disorder.* Chapel Hill, NC: Algonquin Books of Chapel Hill.

Miché, Mary. 2002. *Weaving Music into Young Minds.* Albany, NY: Delmar Thomson Learning.

Nicholson, Simon. 1971. "How NOT to Cheat Children: The Theory of Loose Parts." *Landscape Architecture* 62:30–34.

Oxfordshire Play Association. 2014. "Using Loose Parts for Play." Assessed May 7. www.oxonplay.org.uk/#/loose-parts-for-play/4542808737.

Pepler, Debra J., and Kenneth H. Rubin. 1982. "Current Issues in the Study of Children's Play." *Human Development* 25:443–47.

Piaget, Jean. 1952. *The Origins of Intelligence in Children.* Trans. Margaret Cook. New York: International Universities Press, Inc.

———. 1973. *To Understand Is to Invent: The Future of Education.* Trans. George-Ann Roberts. New York: Grossman Publishers. First published 1948.

Playwork Principles Scrutiny Group. 2005. *Skills Active: The Pocket Guide to Playwork*. Cardiff, Wales: SkillsActive.

Rubin, Kenneth H. 1982. "Nonsocial Play in Preschoolers: Necessary Evil?" *Child Development* 53:651–57.

Shonkoff, Jack P., and Deborah A. Phillips, eds. 2000. *From Neurons to Neighborhoods: The Science of Early Childhood Development*. Washington, DC: National Academy Press.

Singer, Dorothy G., Roberta Michnick Golinkoff, and Kathy Hirsh-Pasek, eds. 2006. *Play = Learning: How Play Motivates and Enhances Children's Cognitive and Social-Emotional Growth*. New York: Oxford University Press.

Sluss, Dorothy Justus. 2005. *Supporting Play: Birth through Age Eight*. Clifton Park, NY: Thomson Delmar Learning.

Smilansky, Sara. 1968. *The Effects of Sociodramatic Play on Disadvantaged Preschool Children*. New York: John Wiley & Sons, Inc.

Vygotsky, Lev. 1967. "Play and Its Role in the Mental Development of the Child." *Soviet Psychology* 5 (3): 6–18.

White, Randy, and Vicki Stoecklin. 2014. "Children's Outdoor Play & Learning Environments: Returning to Nature." Accessed May 8. www.whitehutchinson.com/children/articles/outdoor.shtml.